SpringerBriefs in Economi

C000154703

SpringerBriefs present concise summaries of cutting-edge research and practical applications across a wide spectrum of fields. Featuring compact volumes of 50 to 125 pages, the series covers a range of content from professional to academic. Typical topics might include:

- A timely report of state-of-the art analytical techniques
- A bridge between new research results, as published in journal articles, and a contextual literature review
- A snapshot of a hot or emerging topic
- An in-depth case study or clinical example
- A presentation of core concepts that students must understand in order to make independent contributions

SpringerBriefs in Economics showcase emerging theory, empirical research, and practical application in microeconomics, macroeconomics, economic policy, public finance, econometrics, regional science, and related fields, from a global author community.

Briefs are characterized by fast, global electronic dissemination, standard publishing contracts, standardized manuscript preparation and formatting guidelines, and expedited production schedules.

More information about this series at https://link.springer.com/bookseries/8876

Basil Oberholzer

Fighting Global Poverty

Economic Policy Strategies for Developing Countries

 Springer

Basil Oberholzer
Centre for Development and Environment
University of Bern
Bern, Switzerland

ISSN 2191-5504   ISSN 2191-5512   (electronic)
SpringerBriefs in Economics
ISBN 978-3-658-36630-8   ISBN 978-3-658-36631-5   (eBook)
https://doi.org/10.1007/978-3-658-36631-5

"Basil Oberholzer's book makes an important contribution to the understanding of developing countries' economic problems. Only by challenging the theoretical foundations of mainstream economics, as he does, will we be able to truly support those countries".
—*Heiner Flassbeck, Former Director of Division on Globalization and Development Strategies, UN Conference for Trade and Development (UNCTAD)*

"This book provides an outstanding analysis explaining the major reasons of poverty and how to solve the latter in developing economies through relevant policy reforms. Scholars and policy makers in development economics will find this book extremely useful".
—*Sergio Rossi, Full Professor of Macroeconomics and Monetary Economics, University of Fribourg, Switzerland*

Abstract

This book shows the paths developing countries can pursue in order to reclaim their ability to take action and improve people's living conditions in the long term. According to dominant economic theory, markets are the essential engines of growth and poverty reduction in developing countries. However, the track record so far is disappointing. Moreover, poor countries, which are exposed to the dynamics of global capitalism, have little chance to implement alternative development strategies. Policy action for a fairer income distribution or for more public investment runs the risk of being punished by financial markets and capital flight. The book considers key economic foundations and outlines feasible development strategies.

Contents

Chapter 1
Introduction

After the opposition's victory in the pre-elections in Argentina in August 2019, financial markets reacted immediately. The scenario that the opposition's candidate would become the next president and abandon the then-current president's neoliberal policies was the new commonplace. The peso devalued by almost 50% and inflation started spiking. The central bank raised the target interest rate to 75% in a desperate fight trying to make the currency attractive to investors and hence to prevent any further exchange rate depreciation. Rumors of a new government bankruptcy spread. It was the continuation of the crisis one year before when the government had to request a loan from the International Monetary Fund (IMF), the largest in the Fund's history. In turn, the Fund demanded cuts in public spending aiming at stabilizing the economy and the accumulation of debt. However, lower expenditures imply lower incomes implying that the negative spiral turned on, deteriorating the already more than precarious situation. In 2020, Argentina defaulted on a part of its foreign debt. The country, under the newly elected government, negotiated a debt restructuring with its international creditors in order to prevent a complete default.

As well in 2019, inflation in Venezuela is at several 100'000 percent. Foreign debt continues piling up and debt servicing has to be settled by future oil deliveries due to the lack of foreign currency. Continued currency devaluation makes goods of daily needs unaffordable for the population. The shrinking economy worsens the disaster. The 'Bolivarian Revolution', which had promised transformative economic

---

This book invites an interested audience from the economics profession as well as non-economists. It tries to explain complicated things in the easiest way possible such that readers who are new to the issues discussed here can participate in the debate. Those who want to know more about the economic foundations and details of the analysis are referred to the following more voluminous academic book, which the simplified version at hand is based on: Oberholzer, B. (2020). *Development Macroeconomics: Alternative Strategies for Growth*. Cheltenham and Northampton: Edward Elgar.

change and soon was successful in social development and poverty reduction, has been stopped by a deep economic crisis at least for the time being.

Troubles of this kind are not limited to Latin America. In many African countries, a new debt crisis is looming, revealing bad memories from the 1980s. Back then, capital inflows suddenly stopped, leaving the countries with devalued currencies and high foreign debt. When they defaulted on sovereign debt, governments were forced into privatization of public enterprises and deep cuts in social expenditures by the international finance institutions. As a result, the economies contracted further. The global crisis, which broke out in 2020 due to the coronavirus, might have been the last straw. Several countries in the Global South are currently negotiating on debt restructuring with their creditors.

It seems that poor countries are hit hard regularly by currency and financial crises. Indeed, the consequences of currency devaluation and inflation are devastating as they go along with strong economic contraction and increase in poverty numbers. Such crises destroy economic resources via channels, which are emphasized more in detail throughout this book.

In particular, ambitious progressive policy programs tend to be the victim of the dynamics of global capitalism. Whenever policies intend a redistribution of wealth via market intervention, capital fears a loss of profit. Capital flight sets in and puts devaluation pressure on a country's currency, thereby starting the acceleration of economic trouble. It may not be the only factor to explain the cases of the countries mentioned above. But it represents a serious constraint to any country's development prospects. The restrictions imposed on economic policies by international financial markets is an important reason why the many trials of progressive, left and socialist projects around the world have accumulated to a history of defeats and failures.

Given this experience, one may be tempted to stick to the well-known policy prescriptions for developing countries: minimize the role of the state, privatize public assets, liberalize trade and financial flows, and restrict fiscal and monetary policy to the requirements given by the free-market equilibrium. This recipe was applied in Latin American countries from the 1980s onwards under pressure of international and multilateral financial institutions. However, the results in terms of economic growth were poor. On the other side of the planet, East Asian countries, notably South Korea, Taiwan, Singapore, and a bit later notably China, have achieved lasting success in the fight against poverty by quite a lot of state guidance and intervention.

Yet, the questions remain, and even more so in a time of much less promising global economic performance than during the decades the mentioned East Asian countries started their history of growth: how can countries pursue development strategies if any policy intervention is punished by capital outflows? How can countries get back their scope of action?

This book aims at providing a perspective on this issue. It starts with an overview of global progress in poverty reduction and introduces the central mainstream neoliberal policy recipes for developing countries that are supposed to induce economic prosperity and wellbeing for everyone. This leads us further behind the scene to the arguments in favor of economic deregulation and liberalization. Once the neoclassical model behind mainstream economic thinking is understood, it also becomes clear where its main limits and flaws are. To get a proper idea of how macroeconomics works, we refer to a couple of core principles based on which a dynamic system unfolds. With this much more realistic perception of the economy, it will become clear why mainstream policy recipes do not work. However, this does not make developing countries' problems smaller. They have to act in this complex dynamic space and elaborate policies and strategies that take those dynamics into account.

First, the economy is considered within national borders. It is shown that it is insufficient to leave economic development to market forces. Instead, the government is needed to make use of different policy instruments in order to steer productivity, production capacity and income creation.

However, once we account for the global economy many more complex dynamics enter the stage confronting policies of an individual country. They make active economic policy much less effective and set tight restrictions on poor countries' economic development and growth. Our central aim is to find the right way to reclaim political and economic sovereignty for individual countries making them able to realize effective policies. A reform of the international payment system, which can also be implemented by a single country, is introduced. It stabilizes economic conditions with regard to a country's relationship with the rest of the world. Hence, countries get their scope of action back.

Clearly, this book cannot account for the immense complexity of development macroeconomics. For instance, the focus on economic growth may appear as too limited. Growth is not a sufficient condition for wellbeing, especially as we currently observe inequality of wealth and income distribution becoming more and more unfair. However, growth is a necessary condition to provide the means for lifting poor countries out of misery and material lack (see also Box 2.1).

The further a country moves on its growth path, the more ambiguous the issue of growth becomes. This is why this book ends with a very long-term perspective. It outlines how the policy instruments emphasized here may also be used to relieve society from endless growth—notably with regard to ecological boundaries.

Chapter 2
Are Current Policies on Track to Eliminate Poverty?

Is global poverty declining? Opinions differ. World Bank data support the positive view by measuring the share of population living on a daily income of 1.90 US dollars or less (World Bank 2018). Indeed, according to this benchmark, development policies are successful because only 10% of the world population still have to get along below it. Further indicators such as life expectancy at birth show a rather continuous upward trend (World Bank 2019b). It comes as no surprise that scientists observe that "things are getting better" (see for example Pinker 2018).

However, this optimistic view is countered by several critical arguments. While there are certainly doubts about the measurability of a global poverty line, it is also argued that 1.90 dollars a day are just far too low to sustain a human life. Be it just for the cover of most necessary food expenditures, calculations estimate that at least 5 dollars a day is needed (Lahoti and Reddy 2015, pp. 12–13). According to this benchmark, the number of poor people has clearly increased since 1990—in contrast to what the World Bank poverty line suggests. The most recent report of the UN Food and Agriculture Organization (FAO 2021) also confirms that the number of hungry people has been increasing in five consecutive years from 2014 until 2019. In 2020, the year of the coronavirus pandemic outbreak, the share of people facing food insecurity increased by 5 percentage points, thus the same increase in a single year as in the five previous years combined. In 2020, 118 million more people suffer from hunger than in 2019 (ibid.).

Additionally, progress in poverty reduction is distributed very unequally across continents (World Bank 2019a). Income per capita has grown strongly in East Asia, where China has been the strongest growth engine in the past three to four decades. By contrast, economic growth was far from keeping up with population growth in Sub-Saharan Africa, thus implying a fall in per-capita income since the 1960s. Growth in South Asia, particularly India, has strongly increased since the beginning of this century while in Latin America and the Caribbean growth was somewhere between the rates of Sub-Saharan Africa and South Asia.

However, income is not the only indicator to measure poverty. One may look at literacy rates or health indicators. Let us consider another indicator, which goes

B. Oberholzer, *Fighting Global Poverty*, SpringerBriefs in Economics, https://doi.org/10.1007/978-3-658-36631-5_2

beyond income and provides a good picture of the state of a country's economy. In developing countries, a large fraction of the population is forced to earn a living in the informal sector. It does not guarantee a regular income but is tied to stress, insecurity, and mostly extremely low earnings based on day-to-day chase after business opportunities. The percentage of people in such vulnerable employment has again strongly decreased in East Asia; but it has hardly changed in Latin America, South Asia and Sub-Saharan Africa. From 1991 until 2018, the share in Sub-Saharan Africa declined from about 76 to 72% (World Bank 2019c). So still about three quarters of workers have to work in the informal sector. This is quite disappointing. If we subtract poverty reduction in China from the global numbers, progress in the fight against poverty becomes even more doubtful.

Obviously, poverty is multidimensional and cannot be expressed in a single number. The estimation of income per capita provides limited information on people's actual wellbeing. For instance, it does not say anything about inequality in a society and, related to this, the number of social services provided in a country. Nevertheless, sufficient income in the economy is the very crucial factor to overcome material shortage. Therefore, as critical as its consequences often are, economic growth is a precondition for poverty reduction in developing countries (see Box 2.1).

The utility of growth depends on the extent to which it generates the goods required to serve the population's basic needs. Even though this book mostly takes a macroeconomic perspective where the type of produced goods and services is not defined in detail, it will show how appropriate development strategies are not only able to steer growth but can also promote the particular sectors and industries that are considered as important for society.

Box 2.1 Economic Growth, Poverty and Inequality

As mentioned, there are many well-known indicators to measure progress in poverty reduction such as, for example, infant mortality, the share of under-nourished people in a country, the share of population below a certain income threshold, literacy, and expectancy of life. Any general economic reasoning makes clear that a country needs economic and financial resources to achieve good indicator values and thus a decline in poverty. From a specifically macroeconomic perspective, the most basic interest is in the question about how these resources can be provided. This inevitably leads us to the issue of economic growth.

Economic growth simply means that a country increases the pool of its available resources consisting of consumption goods and investment goods, which can either be the output of markets or provided by the government. First, however, there is a lot of criticism of the definition of gross domestic product, particularly as it does not cover many items and aspects that are of fundamental importance to human wellbeing such as a healthy environment.

(continued)

Box 2.1 (continued)

Second, the growth rate of a country's economy does not necessarily tell us how well every resident is doing materially. Growth may not contribute to poverty reduction if additional incomes are captured by the richest households leaving the vast majority of the population at the same income level.

The issue of income and wealth inequality is particularly important because it has an impact not only on people's relative but also absolute wellbeing. Empirical research provides comprehensive evidence that more unequal societies are more prone to violence, drug abuse and even mental illness (Wilkinson and Pickett 2017). Moreover, these societies produce a lot of economic waste since people spend more on status consumption and security, which itself is required to protect the wealthy against violence and to maintain unequal wealth distribution. All these harmful impacts of inequality are not reflected in growth numbers.

Nonetheless, while economic growth is not a guarantee to eliminate poverty in developing countries, it is a precondition. Without growth, there is a lack of economic resources out of which wealth can be generated and distributed. As an example, take food availability. In 2017, average food supply in Madagascar was about 1900 calories per capita and day (FAO 2017) even though the average requirement is at least 2500 calories. More equal distribution of available food would certainly set many Malagasy better off. However, given that the average of available calories is too low, it would not eliminate the problem of undernourishment. If Madagascar, a particularly poor country, is to provide its population with sufficient food and if it does not want to rely on foreign aid to fund food imports forever, there are only two options. The country must either produce more food on its own or produce other goods the export of which can pay for imported food. In both cases, the Malagasy economy must grow.

The extent to which economic growth is able to effectively reduce poverty differs between countries. An exemplary study by Fosu (2017) investigates the relationship for a broad set of countries between the mid-1990s and the mid-2000s. Poverty measured by daily income thresholds of 1.90 and 2.50 US dollars (though this indicator is far from perfect), respectively, fell quite strongly in countries such as China, Thailand, Tunisia, Costa Rica, and Uruguay while the economy grew. In India, by contrast, poverty reduction was moderate despite continuous strong economic growth, thus denoting an increase in inequality. In Bangladesh, poverty rates even increased despite economic growth. We thus see that inequality significantly affects the contribution of economic growth to poverty reduction. Overall, however, figures in this study also show that growth remains the most important determinant of success in the fight against poverty.

(continued)

Box 2.1 (continued)

Jason Hickel (2019) provides interesting thoughts regarding the relationship between inequality and growth. The World Bank's data on inequality show that incomes of the richest 1% of the world population have increased by 86% from 1980 until 2016. Incomes of the following 49% of people on average increased only by 35% in the same time period. However, since incomes of the poorer half of world population grew by an average of 78%, it can still be argued that global inequality declined despite the strong gains of the top 1%. Yet, this good message is turned into its opposite when absolute instead of relative numbers are considered. The poorest 10% saw their yearly incomes increase by 193 US dollars from 1980 until 2016. The next 10% face income growth of 716 US dollars. By contrast, the richest 1% enjoyed an increase of 124,897 US dollars while the following 9% received an additional 13,739 US dollars. Overall, it is obvious that almost all growth in global income went to the rich and richest in comparison to which increases with all other income classes were negligible. The decline in inequality, which is a relative measure, thus can give rise to misleading conclusions. Global economic growth was mostly at the favor of rich households, while the slight reduction in inequality in the long period of 36 years did not change much about the fact that too many households are caught at income levels of a few US dollars per day.

On the other hand, this analysis confirms that if global inequality is to decline significantly such that low incomes catch up to high incomes, it means that the economies of poor countries have to grow faster than the advanced economies (while inequality within those countries should not increase further). The importance of growth thus remains paramount. Hence, even though this book does not address the issue of inequality directly, it emphasizes it at least indirectly by comparing the purpose of economic growth in developing countries to its role in high-income countries (see Chap. 9).

Since the early 1990s, development economics has been dominated by an agenda called the Washington Consensus. The economist John Williamson summarized what he supposed to be the view of the experts in Washington, including the international finance institutions such as the IMF and the World Bank (Williamson 2004–5). The Consensus is a quite comprehensive set of neoliberal policy recommendations. In short, it proposes budgetary discipline to governments in developing countries. Public spending should be concentrated on health, education and infrastructure. Consequently, state intervention in other sectors is to be limited. Low tax rates are better than high rates. Public enterprises should be privatized. International trade should be liberalized by cutting down tariffs, while the exchange rate is to be set at a competitive level to promote exports. Barriers to market entry and exit need to be abolished. The financial sector should be liberalized with the final objective of interest rates being determined by the market. Therefore, monetary policy is not allowed to depress the interest level to pursue political goals. The building-up of domestic financial markets supports efficient discovery of prices and also interest rates that appropriately reflect market conditions. With regard to the rest of the world, financial flows should be deregulated, notably flows of foreign direct investment (FDI).

Due to continuous criticism, the Washington Consensus got an amendment in the noughties. In particular, it allowed for more space for fiscal policy and anticyclical spending as well as some degree of social income redistribution. Thus, the government was allowed to partially take a more active role in the economy. Moreover, the Consensus emphasized institutional reforms to improve the guarantee of property rights and regulation. However, the its baseline where the market is the institution to solve all economic problems of developing countries remained the same.

The Consensus agenda was applied to Latin American countries after they had experienced currency crises and debt crises in the 1980s. After its disappointing results in terms of economic growth, its proponents became more cautious. Yet, the central ideas of the Consensus are still at the core of development debates and represent the cornerstones of mainstream economics. Let us therefore briefly explain what the most important issues on the neoliberal agenda entail and what their (suggested) economic effects are. We will come back to them in more detail later on.

Restrictive fiscal policy, balanced budget and privatization of public assets pursue one general aim. The role of the state is perceived as the provider of a framework supporting market efficiency. Hence, public intervention in the economy should be reduced in order to increase the degree of competition, fostering international competitiveness, attracting foreign capital, and thereby promoting technological progress. The government should only exceptionally run deficits. Since permanent deficits have to be financed by debt, they induce an oversupply of money, which translates to additional demand. Finally, inflation increases. Economists do not like inflation mainly because it distorts price signals and, consequently, resource allocation. This implies inefficiencies and a waste of resources. In the case of hyperinflation, economic activities may even break down.

Trade liberalization points even more directly to the central stance of mainstream economics. It is justified by David Ricardo's (1817/2001, pp. 85–103) theory of comparative advantage. The idea of the nineteenth-century classical economist states that trade maximizes welfare because it allows every country to produce what it is best at. Economies of scale can be exploited because the countries focus their activities on the sector where their relative production costs are lowest. International exchange of goods is efficient. Firms get access to input material at lower costs while consumers enjoy a higher variety of goods at even lower prices.

Trade also helps technology spill over country borders, thereby supporting knowledge transfer. Protectionism in the form of tariffs, subsidies or entry and exit barriers comes at economic costs because it prevents the efficient allocation of resources. Inefficiency means that investment is made in sectors where another country would be more competitive while other sectors where the country could be an international leader are correspondingly neglected. The country's limited resources are wasted due to missing price signals.

Important to understand is that liberalization of trade is also argued to be an instrument to balance trade so that neither of the trading countries incurs a trade deficit in the long term. Following Ricardo again, in a situation where the exports of a country yield less returns than what it spends for imports, a trade deficit emerges. To pay for those imports, demand for foreign currency increases relative to demand of the domestic currency. The latter thus depreciates. As a result of this, the country's exports become more competitive while imports become more expensive. Increasing exports and falling imports allow the country to rebalance its trade balance. Balanced trade thus is an equilibrium established by market forces.

Finally, financial liberalization aims to increase efficiency in the financial sector along the same principle as trade liberalization. The interest rate equilibrates savings and investment. It is the price at which savers are willing to provide savings for the investment demanded. The equilibrium rate thus is driven by market forces. With the latter reflecting preferences of wealth owners and investors, the equilibrium ensures efficient allocation of resources because it gives rise to the optimal amount of investment. The central bank should therefore not disturb this equilibrium by pushing the interest rate to a different level. This would direct investment to sectors with low profitability (a sign of inefficiency), which could not survive at a higher interest rate. The market rate ensures that capital is employed efficiently.

The same applies to the international level. Better than only at a national level, the optimal equilibrium in the financial market should be established internationally. Like this, first-best capital allocation can be achieved globally instead of merely within the limits of a national economy where capital may be either too scarce or too abundant relative to the rest of the world. Hence, capital should be mobile so that it can find its most profitable investment. For savings and investment to equilibrate globally, countries should not prevent financial flows from either flowing in or out of a national economy. Otherwise, the national interest rate would deviate from the global one, which reflects a distortion. In particular, savings in a developing country are likely to be scarce. Opening up the domestic financial market attracts foreign capital that can be invested in the most efficient way, that is, in the sector where it generates highest returns.

In the more recent past, the mainstream paradigm of unregulated markets has been complemented with an emphasis on the role of institutions. Institutions should be effective bodies for regulation and supervision. As Acemoglu and Robinson (2012, pp. 79–83), the most prominent proponents of the mainstream institutions approach, argue, institutions should be inclusive. By definition, this is given if they protect property rights and promote competition in the market. Inclusive institutions are necessary to guarantee economic prosperity.

This whole development policy agenda was not without impact. State enterprises were privatized in large numbers since the 1980s. Tariffs in basically all world regions have decreased during the past 30 to 40 years (UNCTAD 2018). Likewise, financial liberalization was implemented by removing capital controls in developing countries, thus abolishing regulation of capital inflows and outflows. At the same time, their banking sectors were liberalized. In the meantime, the debate on the appropriate speed and sequence of liberalization steps has become more intense as a result of the disappointing experiences made with past liberalization measures. Regarding institutions, development finance is more tied to criteria of 'good governance' now than it was before the institutions approach received attention (see for instance Kaufmann 2005).

Even though simplified, we now know the essential policy recommendations as made by the World Bank, the IMF, the World Trade Organization (WTO) and other multilateral institutions. They are the cornerstones of a comprehensive economic framework. Let us take one step back and have a look at neoclassical theory, which lays the foundation of mainstream macroeconomics.

References

Acemoglu D, Robinson JA (2012) Why nations fail: the origins of power, prosperity, and poverty. Profile Books, London

Food and Agriculture Organization (FAO) (2021) The State of Food Security and Nutrition in the World: Transforming Food Systems for Food Security, Improved Nutrition and Affordable Healthy Diets for All. https://www.fao.org/documents/card/en/c/cb4474en. Accessed 20 Nov 2021

Food and Agriculture Organization of the United Nations (FAO) (2017) New food balances. http://www.fao.org/faostat/en/#data/FBS. Accessed 20 Nov 2021

Fosu AK (2017) Growth, inequality, and poverty reduction in developing countries: recent global evidence. Res Econ 71:306–336. https://doi.org/10.1016/j.rie.2016.05.005

Hickel J (2019) How bad is global inequality, really? https://www.jasonhickel.org/blog/2019/3/1/global-inequality-from-1980-to-2016. Accessed 30 Nov 2021

Kaufmann D (2005) Back to basics – 10 myths about governance and corruption. Finance Dev 42(3). https://www.imf.org/external/Pubs/FT/fandd/2005/09/basics.htm

Lahoti R, Reddy S (2015) $1.90 per day: what does it say? Institute for New Economic Thinking. https://www.ineteconomics.org/perspectives/blog/1-90-per-day-what-does-it-say. Accessed 30 Nov 2021

Pinker S (2018) Enlightenment now: the case for reason, science, humanism, and progress. Viking, New York

Ricardo D (1817/2001) On the principles of political economy and taxation. Kitchener, Batoche Books

UNCTAD (2018) Import tariff rates on non-agricultural and non-fuel products. http://unctadstat.unctad.org/wds/ReportFolders/reportFolders.aspx. Accessed 24 Oct 2020

Wilkinson RG, Pickett KE (2017) The enemy between us: the psychological and social costs of inequality. Eur J Soc Psychol 47:11–24. https://doi.org/https://doi.org/10.1002/ejsp.2275

Williamson J (2004–5) The strange history of the Washington consensus. J Post Keynesian Econ 27(2):195–206.

World Bank (2018) Decline of Global Extreme Poverty Continues but Has Slowed: World Bank. Press Release NO 2019/030/DEC-GPV. https://www.worldbank.org/en/news/press-release/2018/09/19/decline-of-global-extreme-poverty-continues-but-has-slowed-world-bank. Accessed 14 Jun 2020

World Bank (2019a) GDP per capita growth (annual %). World Bank Indicators. https://data.worldbank.org/indicator/NY.GDP.PCAP.KD.ZG?view=chart. Accessed 24 Oct 2020

World Bank (2019b) Poverty headcount ratio at $1.90 a day. World Bank Indicators. https://data.worldbank.org/indicator/SI.POV.DDAY?locations=1W&start=1981&end=2015&view=chart. Accessed 15 Nov 2020

World Bank (2019c) Vulnerable employment, female/male (% of female employment). World Bank Indicators. https://data.worldbank.org/indica-tor/SL.EMP.VULN.FE.ZS?view=chart and https://data.worldbank.org/indica-tor/SL.EMP.VULN.MA.ZS?view=chart. Accessed 24 Oct 2020

Chapter 3
How Mainstream Economics Works

As the first feature, neoclassical economics relies on individual preferences.[1] Individuals have tastes and needs according to which they make decisions on what to purchase and consume as well as what amount of labor hours to supply in the labor market. Those preferences are expressed by a utility function. As rational personalities, individuals maximize this utility function, which is tantamount to saying, in less mathematical terms, that they make choices in order to maximize their wellbeing. At the macroeconomic level, individuals are usually reflected by one single agent. The so-called representative agent maximizes a representative utility function, which is supposed to represent all individual utilities. In the same vein, it could be said that all individuals have the same utility function. Neoclassical theory has its roots in microeconomics, which explains why such individual behavior is linearly transferred to the aggregate, that is, the macroeconomic level. Such 'micro foundations' of macroeconomics are commented as a methodological strength of neoclassical theory. Indeed, macroeconomics thus is not a nebulous science but can be traced back to and be justified by the analysis at the level of individuals.

In addition to consumers, there are firms. They produce with a certain technology where capital goods and labor are used as production inputs. The technology not only reflects a specific productivity level, it also determines the proportion at which capital and labor are employed. In analogy to the utility function with consumers, the production technology is expressed as a production function. Profits are to firms what utility is to individuals. Hence, firms want to maximize profits. This setting describes a single firm. Again, the production function is transferred to the macroeconomic level where it is assumed that it represents all firms in the economy. The underlying assumption is that all firms have the same production function. At the microeconomic level, they are in competition with each other, which implies maximum output. This result is also directly transferred to the macro level by

---

[1]For a comprehensive critique of neoclassical theory, see for instance Bénicourt and Guerrien (2008).

assumption. Profit maximization of the representative firm shows the optimal amount of output, the optimal levels of the capital stock and employment, as well as optimal interest rate and wage.

The representative agent constitutes the demand side in the goods market while the representative firm is the supply side. Maximization of utility and profits, respectively, determines output, consumption, interest rate, wage, employment, and the capital stock. The combined result of all this is called 'general equilibrium'. Math can be quite complicated when the equilibrium is calculated. The framework can be extended depending on what the researcher wants to analyze. For example, it may have a greater emphasis on the labor market. Alternatively, it may describe the process of investment and capital accumulation over time. In other versions, the goods market can be divided into different sectors; monetary or fiscal policy may play a role; or one can imagine a set of different utility functions. The basic rationale of the theory remains the same.

The most important features of neoclassical theory, derived from these basic assumptions, are the following ones:

- The general equilibrium is optimal because it maximizes welfare. It is achieved autonomously if individuals and firms are free to maximize utility and profits, respectively.
- Full employment always prevails. Any unemployment is voluntary in the sense that individuals prefer not to work at the given wage level.
- Production capacity is always fully utilized.
- As part of optimization, agents also decide what share of output to consume and what to save. Savings turn into investment and increase the capital stock.

Economic activity takes its course along these lines. Changes happen in the form of shocks. For example, there may be an innovation, which replaces hitherto production technology by a new and better one. This increases output in general but may also change the proportion of capital and labor as production inputs. This has, again, an influence on the wage rate and capital return. Continuous utility and profit maximization thus imply a new equilibrium when conditions change. Positive productivity shocks are beneficial to the economy because they are wealth-increasing. In a similar vein, a shock may come from government or monetary policy intervention. Their main effect, however, is that they distort the welfare-maximizing market equilibrium. They are, basically, harmful. This does not mean that there is no role at all for policies. When there is another harmful exogenous shock, monetary and fiscal policy may intervene in a counteracting way that brings the economy back to the optimal equilibrium. This is especially relevant when it is assumed, as a better approximation to reality, that there are time lags preventing immediate adjustment of the equilibrium, and hence causing temporary unemployment.

In the long term, however, policy intervention is ineffective even in this case. Let us imagine that the central bank wants to conduct expansive monetary policy in order to increase economic production. With regard to the role of money, neoclassical economics is largely based on the quantity theory of money. It was introduced to the overall framework mainly by Milton Friedman (see for instance Friedman

1956). According to the quantity theory, known as monetarism, expansive monetary policy means that the central bank provides more money to the economy. A higher money supply provides the means to exert more demand in the market place. One may be tempted to believe that higher demand induces higher production. Yet, more money does not change anything about the real fundamental data of the economy. The production function is not altered in any regard because there is no change in production technology. Thanks to maximization of utility and profits, the economy is already producing at its optimum. There is only one result for expansive monetary policy: higher demand while supply of goods is constant merely translates into higher prices. Supplying more money is an illusion because it just gives way to inflation. Therefore, demand is only increased in nominal terms, that is, in terms of monetary units. But the increase is not real because it does not move the real forces like production factors or technology.

Since there are usually time lags, monetary policy may have temporary effects since it takes time for the economy to realize that higher demand is only driven by more money instead of higher real income. But in the long run, there is inflation, which is harmful because it distorts resource allocation. Since the economy is optimally determined by production capacity on the supply side, the only thing monetary policy can do is providing the right quantity of money that is needed for the economy to run at this optimal level. Since the general equilibrium is inherently stable, it follows that inflation must stem from too expansive monetary policy. Hence Friedman's famous aphorism that "money is always and everywhere a monetary phenomenon" (see for instance Mishkin 2007, p. 2). The same inflationary consequences apply to government budget deficits when they are financed by increasing money supply via the central bank.

After this short introduction, we understand the theory behind recommendations such as budgetary discipline, privatization of public companies, trade liberalization, and financial liberalization. They have in common that they aim to ensure the efficient general equilibrium by either enforcing competition, enabling unrestricted maximization of utility and profits, or preventing inflation. The whole rationale is derived from behavior of individuals and firms at the microeconomic level whereas the government cannot make any significant meaningful contribution to economic development.

Let us examine if the neoclassical framework is an appropriate and realistic description of the economy in the world we live in.

References

Bénicourt E, Guerrien B (2008) La théorie économique néoclassique: microéconomie, macroéconomie et théorie des jeux, 3e éd. La Découverte, Paris

Friedman M (1956) The quantity theory of money: a restatement. In: Studies in the quantity theory of money. University of Chicago Press, Chicago, pp 3–21

Mishkin FS (2007) Will monetary policy become more of a science? National Bureau of Economic Research Working Paper, No. 13566. https://www.nber.org/papers/w13566

Chapter 4
Basic Principles to Understand Macroeconomics

Walking through the streets of one of the big cities in developing countries gives a picture of sceneries like this one: marketeers present their goods for sale either on the floor or on tables. They range from agricultural produce from the city's surrounding area via snacks (often in tiny quantities) to second-hand mobiles, watches, music copies, and second-hand clothes. Some sellers only have a handful of sugar candies or pencils to offer. Second-hand clothes tend to be at the upper end and show the business of the traders who are better off. This scenery is quite a perfect market. It can easily be observed that all bananas have the same price and it is certain that changes in banana supply immediately lead to price adjustment throughout the whole street market. Price discovery thus is efficient. It seems like we are at a kind of general equilibrium with respect to supply of and demand for bananas. The same can be argued for all other goods even if adjustment of prices may sometimes take a bit longer. The market only sells what consumers want, which is the result of the latter maximizing utility. Market efficiency ensures that things, which nobody purchases, are not supplied.

Standing at the market from early morning to evening is a hard job. It involves bargaining, persistence and paying attention so that nothing gets stolen. This is what profit maximization on the seller's side requires. Obviously, this is a competitive market. As such, it should not be disturbed by intervention, wrong regulation and the like.

Our insights into neoclassical economics tell us that this market moves on its optimal path. Needless to say, however, most marketeers are poor and so are most customers. Daily income that can be earned on the market is terribly low and uncertain as we are describing a classical example of the informal sector. Incomes spent by consumers are equally low as can be seen from the very cheap and basic goods sold on the market. Moreover, there has not been much change in the structure of such markets. For decades, sellers have been selling the same things and have been exposed to the same hardships of economic struggle, bargaining, competition, and sometimes violence. This procedure repeats millionfold around the globe every day.

© Springer Fachmedien Wiesbaden GmbH, part of Springer Nature 2022
B. Oberholzer, *Fighting Global Poverty*, SpringerBriefs in Economics,
https://doi.org/10.1007/978-3-658-36631-5_4

The description of this scenery raises doubt about whether markets alone can lift people out of poverty. But then where lies the problem? People selling and buying goods in such markets pursue the best option they have. Yet, they remain poor. Either mainstream economics is right meaning that this is actually the best of what people in developing countries can get. Alternatively, it may be that there are flaws in the theory.

A street market serves as a good illustration of the fundamental problem of economic development. And our examination will make clear that the situation can be translated to other sectors. We now want to pursue the following issue: the above situation describes a competitive market. Hence, why are people in developing countries still so poor? To answer this question, a few very key principles of macroeconomics have to be introduced.

4.1   Money

The neoclassical approach to money is a bit strange. It has been explained above how the market equilibrium comes about. Consumers have preferences according to which they make choices while firms produce with a certain technology and inputs of capital and labor. Yet, this whole setting is in real terms, that is, no money is involved. The equilibrium is achieved without money. In monetarism that we have mentioned before, money is emphasized in more detail. Yet, a closer consideration reveals that money only comes second after the optimal equilibrium is established. Hence, the existence of an equilibrium is assumed and then money is added to the model as a mere medium of exchange.

Moreover, money is treated as if it was a commodity that has chosen to be money by definition. This is what is familiar to us because in history, gold often was treated as a kind of money. This is why, according to mainstream theory, the role of the central bank is to regulate the money supply. When there is too much of this money commodity, its price falls, which means inflation. Even though money is not material nowadays, monetary policy controls its quantity by the supply of reserves to commercial banks, which can relend those reserves to borrowers.

As introduced above, in the neoclassical model agents also decide on savings and investment via utility and profit maximization. At the equilibrium, savings and investment are equated by an equilibrium interest rate, the so-called natural rate. Needless to say, this rate is optimal because it belongs to the general equilibrium. The so-called natural rate reflects the optimal allocation of resources in real terms, that is, in a world without money.[1] The natural rate thus cannot be observed in reality because any interest rate can only be expressed in monetary terms. According to mainstream theory, monetary policy should target money supply such that the

---

[1] The theory of the 'natural rate' is based on the analysis of the economist Knut Wicksell (1898/1965).

monetary interest rate, which can actually be observed and influenced, is equal to the invisible optimal natural rate of interest. Researchers try to detect the level of the natural rate by means of complicated econometric analyses. But even with those methods, it remains quite an artificial concept with rather hypothetical results.

In short, in neoclassical economics the central bank determines the quantity of money while the interest rate is determined in the market. There are other approaches to money that are quite different from the monetarist paradigm. It is particularly post-Keynesian economics where money plays an important role. In contrast to what mainstream theory claims, money cannot just be supplied by decision of the central bank. When investigating the origin of money, it is essential to integrate the banking system into the framework.

Money is needed to finance economic activity. In order to get access to money, firms demand loans from commercial banks. Whenever a loan is granted, money is created out of nothing. This insight has far-reaching consequences. First, money is associated with economic production. Without money, no production can take place in a capitalist economy. Likewise, money can assume no purchasing power without production. This shows that the neoclassical model fails in face of reality: it assumes output to be given and 'adds' money to the equilibrium only after.

Second, money is not a commodity. Since it can be created out of nothing, it is not scarce. Third, money creation is driven by demand. It only comes into existence, if economic agents ask for it. Neither the central bank nor commercial banks can determine money supply. Instead, since money is not scarce, money supply can flexibly adjust to money demand. This implies that the amount of money in existence depends on demand for money, which is itself determined by the level of economic activity. This conception is called 'endogenous money' because its creation is an integrated part of the economic process.[2] Thereby, it marks a contrast to neoclassical theory where money is inserted as a fixed quantity from outside, thus called 'exogenous money'.

Accepting that money is created upon demand is quite different from the main-stream view that too large a money supply is the root of inflation. Money is required to make payments. When wages and prices are high, more money is needed to enable the same number of transactions. By contrast to the mainstream view, money does not drive prices, but prices drive money creation. Thus, money is a result of inflation rather than its cause.

Since money is driven by demand that cannot be controlled by monetary policy, there is only one variable, which can be determined by the central bank: the interest rate. As another difference of the concept of money endogeneity to neoclassical theory, short-run interest rates (which more or less translate into long-term market

---

[2]More on endogenous money can, for instance, be found in Moore (1988).

rates) are set by monetary policy while the amount of money is determined by the market.[3]

By altering the interest rate level, the central bank seeks to influence the economy. Expansive policy is implemented by cutting the interest rate. The intention of a lower interest rate is to reduce firms' production costs such that they have an incentive to increase investment and production. This does not necessarily lead to inflation. Wages do not increase strongly when there is unemployment. Goods prices do not rise either when production capacity is not fully used. As long as there is neither full employment nor capacity utilization at its maximum, additional demand in the market can be satisfied without rising prices. On the other hand, it should be said that lower interest rates may not be sufficient to improve economic performance. When the economy is too depressed, demand for money might not increase significantly even though lower interest rates try to make investment conditions better. A string can be pulled but it cannot be pushed.

Whenever a firm is granted a loan, which it spends for, say, material inputs or wages, the money flow becomes someone's income. The payee receives the money on her deposit as savings. It may be surprising: savings are not the origin of expenditures for production; they are rather the outcome of it. We thus get another important insight. It is not that savings allow for investment. Instead, investment generates its own savings. This is very important because it means, especially in the context of poor countries, that people do not have to save more so that investment can be made to enable economic development. Where there is no income, nothing can be saved. The opposite is true: investment expenditures are required to steer development and they will give way to savings. The latter are not a prerequisite.

4.2   Production, Not Only Exchange

Another thing ignored by mainstream theory is the path money and credit follow. Let us start from scratch. The case considered here is clearly simplified but it shows the essential features. Any productive economic activity begins with a loan granted to the firm. The firm uses the received money to pay wages to its workers. Workers become the owners of the bank deposit, which came into existence due to credit creation. In the production process where workers are employed, output is produced. The firm sells output to consumers who are the workers. They spend their wages for it. The firm uses the sales return to pay back the loan. This process describes a *circuit of money*.[4] Money is created to finance production; and it is destroyed once the

---

[3]It should be said that by now mainstream economics also has approached this view in an approach called the 'new consensus' in monetary policy. Yet, it still largely sticks to the neoclassical framework.

[4]The idea of the monetary circuit is used by post-Keynesian economics but also Marxian approaches or the theory of money emissions. See for example Parguez and Seccareccia (2000).

economic process is completed by consumption. This is possible thanks to the endogeneity of money. Neither are savings a prerequisite nor is the monetary circuit constrained by limited money supply. As long as the bank considers the borrower as creditworthy, it provides the loan at the rate of interest broadly defined by monetary policy.

Of course, in our world there is not only credit for production. Loans may also be provided for consumption expenditures or investment in financial markets. Moreover, there is interest, which firms also have to pay for the loans they receive. There are further issues such as firms' own profits and the specific characteristics of the production of investment goods compared to consumption goods. Yet, the monetary circuit can incorporate these extensions (not at this place, though) and remains a robust concept to understand the macroeconomy.

The monetary circuit points to a feature, which is essential to have an appropriate idea of the dynamics of a capitalist economy. Namely, it describes a production process. This is missing in neoclassical theory. There we have a production function. The level of output is determined *a priori* because production capacity is fully utilized and there is full employment as well. In the market, then, exchange takes place as firms, or the representative firm, respectively, sell output to consumers. This exchange is well known from the diagrams where supply and demand curves cross. However, exchange is not everything. It is only one section of the monetary circuit and of the whole economic process. Whereas our enhanced approach starts with the granting of a loan, payment of wages and production, supply of goods is already given in the neoclassical framework by the production function and the general equilibrium. In the circuit, the loan is repaid after exchange has taken place. This last step is again missing in the mainstream model.

John Maynard Keynes (1933/1973) pointed out this difference: the neoclassical model is a mere economy of *exchange*. An appropriate analysis requires a more comprehensive consideration. The monetary circuit therefore describes a monetary economy of *production*. Once this difference is understood, it is easy to see that the framework of the economic mainstream breaks down. Since the role of the monetary circuit in the production process is essential, an economy of production is always *monetary*, hence another difference to the *real* economy of exchange.

When an entrepreneur starts a new business, or plans the next year of his existing activities, he has to decide on how much to produce. If the plans are ambitious, more workers are hired. Therefore, the entrepreneur needs a higher loan than if the number of workers was lower.[5] From this, we can already see two important aspects: the entrepreneur's planning of production implies that the amount of output can vary from year to year. Hence, it is by no means clear that his equipment, that is, his production capacity, is fully utilized permanently. It is only in some moments that he produces at his maximum potential. Since the number of employed workers varies as

---

[5] One may argue that no loan is needed at all because the firm uses past profits to pay the wages with. It can be shown that from a macroeconomic perspective, the problem nonetheless comes down to the one described here.

well, there is no reason to claim that there is permanent full employment. Knowing that all firms have to make decisions on the same questions, it is actually rather the rule than the exception that there is unemployment. It is needless to point to the situation in developing countries where unemployment is very high so that too many people have to struggle for survival in the informal sector. Since the number of workers employed is decided by the entrepreneur, it is rather illogical to claim that any resulting unemployment is voluntary. Yet, this is what mainstream theory does.

Now, how does an entrepreneur decide on how many workers to employ? This can be understood by the fundamental principle of *effective demand* as developed by Keynes (1936/1997, p. 55). The firm tries to estimate the sales returns by end of the coming year. If the entrepreneur thinks that he will be able to sell a lot, he employs more workers, otherwise he employs less. He knows that the potential of returns depends on the state of the total economy, which can by and large not be influenced by himself. So what he can do is to observe the market and build expectations. He tries to guess how many workers the firms in the rest of the economy are going to employ. The higher total employment, the more income is created and the more our particular entrepreneur will be able to sell. That is, the higher effective demand will be.

Unfortunately, he is not the only one who tries to guess what the future will bring. All other firms do likewise. Everyone builds expectations on what all others are going to do. We end up with expectations that are mutually dependent. Such expectation-building can potentially go quite far involving that the entrepreneur thinks about what the other firms expect him to expect and since they do likewise, he may even try to guess what the other firms expect him to expect what they expect what he expects and so on... The key point is that agents act according to their expectations. They may be initially wrong. But expectations are not only based on guesses about reality, but actually create reality even though this creation will not necessarily be what the agents' wish for. Expectation building is so complex that it cannot be traced by any mathematical procedure. The economy thus is subject to *uncertainty*, which is another important concept of Keynes (1937).

Given this complexity, the firm tries to estimate effective demand based on experience. If all produced goods could be sold last year, the business seems to run well. More workers can be hired. If, however, sales did not go well so that inventories had to be accumulated, the firm will cut down employment for the coming year. Lower employment by this respective firm means that less income can be spent. The decision of this entrepreneur thus contributes to lower demand exerted in the market. Other firms may therefore as well experience worse sales returns so that they also decide to cut down employment. In an environment of uncertainty, such impacts are self-enforcing. Strong effective demand becomes even stronger due to firms' optimistic expectations while weaker demand involves a reduction in employment, thus accelerating economic contraction in the next year.

There is the well-known paradox of thrift that we can explain by the dynamics of effective demand under uncertainty. Not only firms make decision in an uncertain environment, but all agents in the economy. In a certain moment, firms and workers may decide to save a part of their revenues and wages in order to be better prepared when there is an economic recession in the future. Firms purchase less input materials, make less investment expenditures and hire fewer workers while workers make less consumption expenditures. Obviously, effective demand shrinks. As a consequence, firms cut down production plans even more and workers are just the more scared about the future. However, since total output in the economy decreases, less income is created out of which people can save. Total savings are finally lower rather than higher.

We have gained some important insights, which show why neoclassical theory is quite flawed in too many regards:

- Macroeconomic outcomes can be quite different from agents' intentions at an individual level. Therefore, it is impossible to explain macroeconomics by linearly translating individual behavior and preferences from the micro level to the macro level. This is exactly what mainstream economics does. We see that it is wrong.
- Effective demand and uncertainty are crucial elements to understand macroeconomics. They give rise to instability and unforeseen dynamics. In mainstream theory, there is no expectation building.[6] There is not even time at all since the general equilibrium is established by all agents making instantaneous and simultaneous decisions. This is quite far from reality. The dynamics incorporated in the monetary circuit show that there is, in fact, no such thing like a stable general equilibrium.
- Since we know that money is created by granting loans, we also know that investment determines savings rather than the other way around. The paradox of thrift clearly reveals the wrong neoclassical way of thinking. Saving more out of income does not make the economy better but worse off in the future.

Why does mainstream economics fail to see this? Because it is reduced to a world where a general equilibrium is built under unrealistic assumptions making market outcomes perfect. Since output is already given by the general equilibrium, only exchange where supply and demand meet is considered. It does not say anything about the forces, which drive the level of supply and demand. In reality, however, there is much more to account for. There is a money-creating banking system,[7] expectations, planning production, and a production process. Neoclassical theory may tell us something about the efficiency of exchange in markets. But it does not tell us anything about the possible level of employment and output at which such exchange takes place.

---

[6]There are neoclassical models with expectation-building. But there, expectations usually are reduced to different future states with a certain probability for each. This is something quite different from uncertainty as introduced here.

[7]Throughout this book, if not specified differently, by 'banking system' we comprise all banks in the economy including the central bank. Since our focus is not on issues between the different entities within the banking system, this simplification is appropriate. Our interest is mainly in the banking system as the source of credit and money as well as its role in making payments.

4.3 Profitability

Effective demand must be sufficient so that firms are willing to expand production. However, demand is not the only condition. Firms only pursue any economic activity if it is profitable. The profit rate, as measured by the ratio of profit to capital employed, must be sufficient. Capitalism is driven by the search for profit and investment goes to those sectors where the profit rate is highest. Profitability as the law of motion in capitalist economies is one of Karl Marx's central insights in his economic analysis (Marx 1894/2004, pp. 44–45; Shaikh 2016, p. 16). This involves turbulent dynamics. On the one hand, capital moves between different sectors. In a highly profitable sector, more investment increases output so that competition reduces the profit rate via falling prices. In a sector with profitability below average, investment decreases so that the remaining capital gets better returns. This is why there is a tendency for the profit rates in different sectors to equalize.

On the other hand, the average profit rate of the economy as a whole may vary. If profitability falls too low to be interesting for investors and if there are no, or just too few, sectors with sufficient profits, total investment falls and firms cut back production. There is a crisis and the economy contracts.

Total income of the economy can be divided into profits and wages. The higher the wages, the lower the profits. Hence, to keep the profit rate at an acceptable level, firms try to press down wages. This distribution struggle is especially hard when the profit rate is in downturn. The conflict can be cushioned by productivity growth. Higher productivity allows for higher output with inputs remaining the same. It therefore also allows for both higher wages and higher profits such that the profit rate can be maintained.

Neither high effective demand nor a high profit rate is in itself sufficient to bring about economic prosperity. In fact, both are necessary conditions. High demand for goods is useless if production of those goods does not yield a profit because nobody is going to produce them. On the other hand, high profitability is not helpful either if there is a lack of demand at the same time since nobody is going to buy those goods. Profits would be high but they cannot be realized. These two conditions are required in the short term to get an economy out of a recession or depression as well as to increase productivity and growth in the long term. Productivity growth is linked to technological progress and efficiency gains, which come about via investment. Investment itself depends on profitability and effective demand. Hence, since these two conditions cannot be taken as granted, productivity growth also does not take place automatically.

In general, there is a contradiction between the profit rate and effective demand. Rich people save a larger fraction of their income than poor people. The poor usually cannot save at all. Wage incomes thus contribute more to effective demand than profit incomes. A higher share of profits in total income contributes to a higher profit rate but at the same time reduces demand because wages are lower. This is the very fundamental dilemma of capitalism. Strengthening either profits or demand weakens the respective other condition for economic prosperity. As mentioned, the higher productivity growth, the more easily both conditions can be sufficiently satisfied.

Box 4.1 Market Efficiency in Slums?

One billion people live in urban slums. The decades-long global movement from rural areas to cities is further raising their number. Extremely poor housing, sanitary conditions, exposure to natural disasters, violence, and the harshness of informality describe the misery of slum dwellers. In his brilliant book on the global spread of urban slums since the middle of the twentieth century, Mike Davis (2017, pp. 61–69) shows that numerous approaches to lift slum dwellers and miserable squatters out of their precarious circumstances have failed. The most remarkable proposal revealing the thinking of mainstream economics is Hernando de Soto's idea. The Peruvian economist has argued since the 1980s that informality is the essential obstacle to economic prosperity. Slums bear a huge potential of productive forces that goes unused since the slum population misses property rights. Hence, slum dwellers are not able to employ their capital because there is no declared ownership of that capital. Once these people become the official owners of the place they factually occupy, they would start expanding economic activities and investing to further increase their capital stock. This would create jobs and income.

Indeed, the informality of slums often lacks the definition of property rights. Yet, as numerous critics pointed out, slums are not a simple ecosystem where every household occupies a certain piece of land such that the problem can be solved by attributing ownership of land (Davis 2017, pp. 79–82). Most slum dwellers do not live in slums for free. Instead, as poor as the shelters are, people often have to rent them. Moreover, a lot of land is owned by wealthy people living far from the area. While some landowners draw not bad money out of the poor urban areas, the cascade of hierarchies means that in most cases renting means that poor inhabitants of slums exploit even poorer ones. Titling of land comes to the advantage of landowners but may make the majority of renters and squatters even worse off.

Clearly, this approach of economic formalization has a too simplistic view of the political economy of slums. The same applies for its view of economics in general. The de Sotoan argument is basically as follows: economic institutions have to be set up the right way and the rest is done by the market. The right institutions are, of course, well-protected private property rights. As soon as they are defined, the slum dwellers' pursuit of a better life and competition in the marketplace maximize welfare.

The neoliberal approach to slum policy is a good example of mainstream economics' misunderstandings. The assignment of property rights does not change anything about the fact that people's income is low. And where there is

(continued)

Box 4.1 (continued)

no income, there is no demand. Moreover, informal economies mainly consist of manual work. Productivity is quite low. If there were profitable investment opportunities beyond trading, illegal business and land ownership, they would take place even if property rights are not defined on paper. Even where the latter are absent, there are relationships of contracts, power and business in slum areas. There are property rights, even though their definition is informal. Hence, despite informality, the economic opportunities are largely explored. Yet, based on its flawed analysis, the economic mainstream assumes that wealth can be created out of exchange in a competitive environment. In fact, we know that production is required. And significant investment only takes place when the two engines of growth, effective demand and profitability, are sufficient.

References

Davis M (2017) Planet of slums, 3rd edn. Verso, London

Keynes JM (1933/1973) A monetary theory of production. In: Moggridge D (ed) Collected writings of John Maynard Keynes, vol. XIII – The general theory and after, part I – Presentation. Macmillan, London, pp 408–411

Keynes JM (1936/1997) The general theory of employment, interest, and money. Prometheus Books, New York.

Keynes JM (1937) The general theory of employment. Q J Econ 51(2):209–223

Marx K (1894/2004) Das Kapital. Kritik der politischen Ökonomie, dritter Band. Akademie Verlag, Berlin

Moore BJ (1988) Horizontalists and verticalists: the macroeconomics of credit money. Cambridge University Press, Cambridge

Parguez A, Seccareccia M (2000) The credit theory of money: the monetary circuit approach. In: Smithin J (ed) What is money? Routledge, London, pp 101–123

Shaikh A (2016) Capitalism: competition, conflict. New York, Oxford University Press, Crises

Wicksell K (1898/1965) Interest and prices: a study of the causes regulating the value of money. Augustus M. Kelley, New York

Chapter 5
Markets Alone Make No Development

We can now come back to the example of the street market in a big city of a development country that we described above and answer the question why there is no economic development and improvement in living standards. The market may be efficient. But there is a crucial problem: goods are only exchanged while nothing is produced. There are snacks, mobiles, second-hand clothes. But they are all imported.[1] This means in essence that money leaves the country to pay for those things. After that, goods and money change hands. But exchange alone does not produce any wealth, however efficiently this exchange might take place. Supply of goods is not just a given thing as assumed in the mainstream, it involves a production process. For anything to be exchanged, it has to be produced first. Since production and the corresponding dynamics are ignored by neoclassical theory, it is not able to explain why people are poor even though we observe something like a market equilibrium.

The efficient market is not to blame because investment can increase productivity so that wealth increases and people can afford more. This is how one may argue. Indeed, investment in better equipment and new sectors would allow to expand production. But why does investment not take place? Certainly not because people cannot afford the savings to make investments as obviously savings stem from investment. The reason is quite different. Maybe investment is not profitable. And if it is, prospects of sales returns would be doubtful because people are poor and do not have the income to pay for more than they can afford now. This is why no private investor is interested in investing and changing the structure of such a market. Even perfect and strong institutions would not change anything about the situation if the two conditions of growth are not fulfilled.

As we can clearly see, market efficiency alone is not able to change the living conditions of the poor. As long as the growth engines, that is, sufficient profit rate

---

[1] Agricultural goods are an exception as they are produced in the same country in most cases. But their value added is usually rather low.

© Springer Fachmedien Wiesbaden GmbH, part of Springer Nature 2022
B. Oberholzer, *Fighting Global Poverty*, SpringerBriefs in Economics,
https://doi.org/10.1007/978-3-658-36631-5_5

and effective demand, are not in place, an economy remains in its stagnant state. Moreover, and here we also deviate from the mainstream, the general equilibrium state is not a law of nature. Deviation from any hypothetic optimal point does not have to be harmful to welfare. Decisions on investment and the hiring of workers determine total economic performance. There is no determined output level given in advance from which no deviation is allowed, quite in contrast to what neoclassical theory argues. Hence, there is nothing wrong in promoting policies that strengthen both investment and employment creation.

5.1 The Role of Policy Intervention in the Economic System

To fight poverty and raise people's income, the economy needs to become more productive. Productivity growth requires investment. If the market alone cannot guarantee this, what can? On the one hand, there is monetary policy. When talking about the profit rate the sufficiency of which is a condition for investment to take place, we actually mean the net profit rate given by the difference between the profit rate and the interest rate. The higher the interest rate, the higher the fraction of production profits a firm has to forward to the banking system, which has provided credit. Hence, the higher the interest rate, the lower the profits. By lowering the interest rate level, the central bank improves profit prospects of the producing sectors in the economy. Monetary policy thus can contribute more to an improvement in economic activity than the mainstream suggests.

However, a change in the interest rate does not affect the state of effective demand, at least not directly. Moreover, the interest rate is only one component influencing profits. In the common situation of a developing country where economic development has been stagnating for years and decades, it is doubtful that a cut in the interest rate can make the change required. Active monetary policy thus may be useful but most likely insufficient.

The problem is that agents in the market are powerless against macroeconomic dynamics. Making investment expenditures and increasing employment in order to strengthen effective demand is a losing deal if a firm is the only one to do it. Sufficient demand and profitability must be given at an aggregate level. Otherwise, the economy remains stagnant because nobody is willing to invest.

There is one exception to this. One single agent is able to make decisions, which can have a direct impact at the macroeconomic level. Indeed, the state is a macroeconomic agent. Policy decisions are powerful enough such that government economic intervention can shift markets. By contrast to private profit-seeking firms and investors, the government can define political and economic objectives. For instance, such objectives may be poverty reduction, employment or a fairer income distribution. To achieve them, a certain economic development is required. The state thus may increase social spending and finance it by taxes. Or it may even make productive investment and contribute to total output via public sector production. When talking about the simple term 'economic policy' in this context, we mean more than legal regulation. It is not about just providing 'good institutions' to support the efficiency of markets, but rather about the government to get active in the marketplace.

The reason why the state is able to target economic development is actually simple. Its purpose is political rather than the search for profit. Therefore, profitability is not a condition to become active. Instead, if willing, the government can also bear investment projects with zero profits. For a considerable time, it can even afford deficits. This difference to the private sector has crucial consequences. As mentioned, the dilemma of capitalism is that increasing the profit rate tends to weaken demand and vice versa. However, for the economy to grow, both are necessary prerequisites. Since this is true for the private sector but not for the government, the latter can even become active in a situation where there is neither demand nor profitability, as is the case in many parts of developing economies. Thereby, government intervention can fully focus on macroeconomic objectives, that is, on fostering economic development.

There are plenty of sectors and industries the state can target to steer growth in the economy. Many of them, such as infrastructure in transport or energy provision are often not profitable. Nevertheless, they are indispensable for the rest of the economy. Moreover, they raise productivity of the whole economy via different channels. Capital accumulation in the public sector usually goes along with technological improvement, efficiency and knowledge gains much like in the private sector. In particular, public infrastructure lays a foundation for many other sectors to become more productive and profitable. Besides contributing to capital accumulation, investment also creates additional demand because the production of capital goods involves employment, thus giving rise to increasing income. And finally, public equipment and production plants increase total production capacity in the economy. The public sector also contributes directly to economic growth and employment by producing goods.

5.2 How the Mainstream Argues Against Policy Intervention

This short sketch shows how policy intervention by creating demand and production capacity can support economic development. Yet, the arguments against government intervention are at least as familiar to us as those in favor of it. While it is often criticized by groups with material interests who fear higher taxes, there are also reasons rooted in neoclassical theory that are brought forward against it. In particular, there are three main strands of argument suggesting that active economic policy worsens the state of the economy or is useless at best.

The first argument has already been mentioned above. Neoclassical economics considers the general equilibrium to be the first-best outcome. It can only be deteriorated by both monetary and fiscal policy. Individuals make consumption choices, which suit their preferences best. Thanks to allocation signals in the market, the supply side of the economy is able to exactly provide those goods under consideration of the existing production capacity. If a part of these goods is provided by the state instead of the private sector, at best the same welfare can be achieved if the state goods are equal to those the private sector would produce in absence of the state. The potential of fiscal policy thus is quite restricted. And since the government is less bound to price signals, it may easily produce goods that do not meet consumers' needs. The use of economic resources thus is less than optimal.

The term 'fiscal policy' usually means stabilization of the economy in the short to middle term, thus involving anticyclical spending. The interest of this investigation goes beyond this because we argue that the government can not only stabilize output but also promote growth and productivity in the long term by means of active economic policy. This is a perspective the mainstream economic model does not even account for. But we can show that as much as the arguments against fiscal policy suffer from analytical weakness, they do equally with regard to policy intervention in the long term.

The superiority of the market equilibrium against any policy intervention is based on the view that the economy is merely an exchange while total output is taken as given by the existing production capacity (the production function). However, what this argument forgets is that production capacity is not fixed. Investment increases production capacity as has just been explained. The government can contribute to it, which is something unforeseen in mainstream economics. Public investment raises overall capital accumulation in the economy. More capital goods imply, broadly speaking, better technology and therefore higher productivity. Therefore, by increasing capital accumulation and steering productivity growth, the public sector raises total production capacity. Economic policy hence does not mean a distortion of a certain general equilibrium because such an equilibrium is meaningless. Instead, appropriate economic policy improves economic welfare.

The second main argument against active economic policy concerns the claim that the government's finance capacity is constrained. A state may have many tasks but, unfortunately, its funds are limited. For instance, infrastructure in developing countries demands a lot of investment, which the government cannot provide. To accomplish all those needs, the engagement of the private sector is required. This is also another argument in favor of privatization of public enterprises or, at least, private-sector participation in formerly public assets.

Obviously, this view adopts a wrong conception of money. It acts on the assumption that money is limited so that the government cannot overcome financing restrictions. Needless to say, money is created via the granting of loans. There is no a priori constraint for the government to finance the projects it considers as important for economic development.

In response to this, it is argued that the government cannot afford too high a level of debt. Even though the state is a quite particular agent in the economy, it still shares several features with private firms and households. So, it is true that public debt should not grow too high. At a certain level, lenders and purchasers of government bonds start doubting the capability of the state to repay debt in the future. They start demanding higher interest rates to cover the growing default risk.

A particular strand in heterodox monetary theory, which has gained traction in recent years, completely rejects this argument. The so-called modern money theory (MMT) argues that due to money's nature as a product of a credit-based banking system, any public debt can be financed by that same banking system. The government of a country, which is sovereign in issuing its currency, thus can afford any amount of expenditures and drive demand to whatever target level. The only condition to be fulfilled is a stable and sufficiently low inflation rate. As long as inflation is under control, the government can pursue and achieve full employment.[2]

While modern money theory correctly describes the mechanism of the national monetary system, one may still argue that demand is not necessarily sufficient to drive economic activity to any desired level. When the profit rate is in a slump, production does not react to nominal demand exerted by government spending. With output stagnating, higher demand translates into higher prices. Hence, while modern money theory is correct in pointing out that inflation needs to be taken into account, it is precisely the issue, which limits the effectiveness of government spending. It is thus not sufficient to just mention inflation, when inflation is the elephant in the room, which might become relevant very soon in an expenditure program.

Yet, modern money theory, though not emphasizing profitability as a particular engine of growth, has an answer to this problem by suggesting an employer of last resort program. Such a program could be established by the government, which complements the private sector by providing everyone with a job at a certain low wage. This wage therewith becomes the factual minimum wage since no employer would be able to offer employment at lower wages. The identified response to the lack of private sector activity is found in public investment and employment much like in our suggestion here.

Unlimited government spending requires an institutional setting where the central bank is allowed to directly finance government expenditures. However, the current reality in most developing countries, though not its inevitable eternal destiny, is a separation of monetary policy and the government's treasury. There are legal and institutional constraints to unlimited deficit spending. Furthermore, precisely guaranteeing constant full employment by complementing but not compromising the private sector also meets difficulties in practice. This is why our proposal does not necessarily target full employment in the same sense because public sector activity necessarily affects the private sector such that neutral complementarity in precise fine-tuning is hardly possible. Finally, the strongest limit to modern money theory will become clear in the following chapters when we consider the open economy. We will see that due to external constraints, most countries lose full sovereignty over their currencies, which is an essential element to justify modern money theory.

---

[2] For an introduction to modern money theory, see Wray (2015).

Despite several critical aspects of modern money theory (besides its analytical merits) and our lack of space to discuss it in more detail, there are a couple of reasons to argue against debt being an insurmountable obstacle. First, we now know how the monetary system works. To finance production, debt is required. There is no difference in this regard whether production is private or public. When investment increases, total debt exposure of the economy grows at least for a while before returns on investment allow to pay back the debt. Second, public debt does not have to last forever. Consumption expenditures can be funded by taxes. Productive investment involves debt, but it also creates real assets in the form of capital goods, which may for example be production plants or infrastructure. Capital goods usually create a cash flow in the future, which helps repay debt.

Third, in most debates, only gross debt plays a role. Net debt, which is gross debt after the deduction of assets, should also be considered. Investment does not lead to an increase in net debt because the newly created assets increase by the same amount as the loan needed to finance their production. Finally, public debt is mostly measured as a percentage of GDP. The larger economic output, the larger the productive potential out of which debt can be paid back in the future, either through taxes or through increased returns of public investment. To the extent that active economic policy promotes economic growth, the debt ratio does not even necessarily increase.

According to the economic mainstream, too much money creation, this time by the government, increases inflation. If money supply itself is not limited absolutely, then there is at least an implicit finance constraint set by the requirement of price stability. Hence, there should be no deviation from the quantity of money, which corresponds to stable prices. Yet, it has been shown above why money itself is not inflationary. Inflation increases when full employment is achieved so that wages start rising or when production capacity is fully utilized so that firms increase prices to meet higher demand while nobody is willing to increase production capacity due to a lack of profitability.

As regards employment, it should be said that unemployment is one of the main reasons for the government to intervene. Therefore, speaking in a simplified way, when full employment is achieved, no more economic policy is needed. Or it may target those sectors where public investment supports productivity progress, but which are less labor-intensive. With respect to capacity utilization, it is true that higher expenditures create higher demand and tend to increase the utilization rate. But this is only one part of the story because at the same time, investment also increases production capacity itself. It is not that growing demand meets fixed production capacity. Investment involves a dynamic process where higher demand meets higher capacity on the supply side. Inflation caused by economic policy is not a necessity at all.

Instead of blaming the public sector for getting involved in specific sectors, one should rather once again raise the question of why such intervention is necessary. For instance, if there is a suggested investment gap in infrastructure in developing countries (UNCTAD 2014, p. 140), why is it not filled by private investment? The answer is simple once again. While it may not be a problem to find private investors for the energy sector or health care for high-income groups, it is much more difficult to generate private contributions for railways, sanitation or schools and hospitals accessible for everyone. The former generate profits, the latter likely do not. Such infrastructure is of tremendous importance for the whole economy. But insufficient profitability prevents private sector participation. This reveals even more the necessity of the government to push economic development because the market will not do it alone.

5.3 The Private Sector Benefits, Too: Crowding-In

The third argument against public intervention in the market is made by reference to a crowding-out of the private sector. Specifically, it is argued that the more the public sector expands, the more the private sector shrinks. This would be harmful because it would reduce competition as a market principle. The larger weight of the public sector thus reduces innovation and efficiency. Moreover, the public sector can only do so because it has the monopoly power to raise taxes and therefore usually can afford higher debt than private sector firms.

Crowding-out of the private sector is argued to occur through different channels. First, since public sector expansion raises demand for money. Consequently, interest rates increase such that borrowing becomes unaffordable for the private sector. This would indeed be the case if money was limited. But it is not. The amount of money is determined by demand while the general interest rate level is set by the central bank. Higher demand for loans affects money creation but it leaves the interest rate unaltered.

Another channel of crowding-out is suggested to happen due to changes in individual behavior. The so-called Ricardian equivalence states that when there is government spending causing a deficit, households know that this will have to be compensated by a future budget surplus.[3] Hence, an increase in taxes will be inevitable. In anticipation of a higher tax bill, households reduce consumption to save a part of income. The amount of additional demand from the government is exactly compensated by reduced demand of households. Needless to say, this argument has more than one weak point. First of all, the future is uncertain. It is thus not clear when a tax increase takes place and how individuals can anticipate it. Second, the demand stimulus of government expenditures affects production, employment and, eventually, total income. A future tax increase, if even necessary, relies on an expanded tax base and thus weighs less heavy.

A third crowding-out mechanism goes through the labor market. Public spending enhances demand on the labor market giving rise to an increase in wages. Higher wages make production for the private sector more expensive so that production plants are closed. There is some merit to this argument. In contrast to the supply of

---

[3] For a critical view of the Ricardian equivalence, see for example Arestis and Sawyer (2003).

money, the supply of labor does not flexibly adjust to demand for it. Changes in the number of workers occur quite slowly over time and are largely insensitive to demands in the labor market.[4] As long as full employment does not prevail, however, wages do not increase too strongly with higher demand for it. The claim that wages respond immediately to policy intervention is, once again, justified by the assumption that the economy guarantees full employment anyway. The government therefore cannot contribute to higher employment but only crowds out the private sector. Yet, as already argued, high unemployment is exactly the motivation for the state to set up growth-enhancing economic policy programs.

In fact, rather than crowding out the private sector, public intervention can crowd it in. Obviously, public spending creates demand, thus contributing to better sales returns for private firms. Beyond this, appropriate economic policy also increases profitability in the economy. Public investment adds to the capital stock of the economy and thereby makes it more efficient while also fostering technological progress. Productivity increases so that with the same inputs, more output can be produced. Consequently, with the level of wages given, profits grow. The situation for the private sector therefore improves in both dimensions: effective demand strengthens while the profit rate increases. Private investment accelerates in response to public investment; hence the crowding-in.

The overall benefit of economic policy thus is multiplied. We observe a version of the so-called Keynesian multiplier stating that an initial expenditure eventually creates an even higher income, which more than pays off the initial spending. This is also how we can express the different views of the public sector's impact on the economy. In our analysis, the multiplier can well be greater than one. Neoclassical theory suggests that the multiplier is equal to one at best but, due to deviation from general equilibrium, rather smaller than one. In empirical research, this claim is confirmed by the application of structural models. They measure the impact of public spending on private sector performance and control for effects such as higher rates of economic growth or external shocks. In such as setting, however, it is not surprising to find evidence in favor of a crowding-out. Separating the effect of economic growth from the relationship between the private and the public sector means that we assume the pattern of GDP to be fixed with respect to this relationship. The two sectors are allowed to influence each other but only under the condition that the pattern of GDP is given. Like this it is just a necessity to find a shrinking private sector when the public sector expands. Yet, it is precisely via higher economic growth that public sector investment crowds in the private sector.

---

[4]Obviously, this argument is weakened when taking migration into account. In contrast to the analogy with the supply of money, the differences nonetheless remain stark.

5.4   Active Economic Policy for Development

We now have collected the elements for successful economic policy. We have the given situation where developing economies are remaining at extremely low income levels. Believing in efficient markets to raise living standards does not help as we have seen in the discussion above. As long as there is no demand and as long as the important sectors for development are not profitable enough for private investors, the market alone does not alter the miserable state of poor people. The question is less about whether markets are efficient or not, it is about whether efficiency is enough. It is not. What is mainly needed is productive capacity rather than simply efficient exchange. Economic policy comes in here. Its most important task is not guaranteeing efficiency as suggested by the mainstream (even though we do not say it has no importance). Instead, policy must be employed to increase productivity and production capacity, which otherwise do not develop. Appropriate public spending and investment plans push the limits.

In designing policy intervention, a government needs to take account of the characteristics of different types of expenditures. Consumption expenditures can be used to make social transfers to poor households. Those households hardly save any income so that the transfers directly translate into additional demand. Funding of public consumption spending by taxes needs to consider certain aspects. Taxes withdraw demand from the market and therefore, the higher the deficit, the stronger the demand impulse. To the extent that taxation is progressive in wealth and income, rich households pay more than the poor. Thereby, public spending still makes a demand impulse even if there is no deficit since social transfers from rich to poor households reduce saving while increasing consumption.

On the other hand, such taxation reduces income out of profits and thus, in general, the profit rate. The positive impact of a budget-neutral demand stimulus on economic growth is therefore ambiguous because it is not clear how private investment finally reacts. For this reason, deficit-financing has a stronger effect. Tax income may increase later on when the economic base has expanded. Yet, the level of debt a government can afford at a given moment is limited. More on this is going to follow.

This is why economic policy via directly making productive investment has a larger potential to raise economic growth. Our conclusions refer to what is known as industrial policy. Priority should be given to the productive base because it determines the amount of wealth, which can be created. In particular, it is manufacturing where highest productivity gains can be realized from which the rest of the economy benefits thanks to spillovers. Public sector investment expenditures not only induce the private sector to expand production indirectly via accelerating demand, they also add directly to the economy's capital stock. Employment is already generated when investment is made and even more so when the public sector starts using the enlarged production capacity.

We have argued that depending on economic performance, private firms increase or reduce both employment and capacity utilization. Since the government does not have to obey the profitability imperative, it can maximize capacity utilization. Producing at full capacity (or leaving a certain flexibility margin) also allows to maximize employment. In this regard, the state may be more efficient than the private sector. Full capacity utilization means the most efficient use of available resources.

Indeed, inflation is an issue economic policy should take account of. For the reasons explained, a demand stimulus given by government expenditures may possibly raise inflation. Then it might not be appropriate to enlarge the policy program further. On the other hand, inflation can also be an indicator of an accelerating economy. In this case, fighting inflation by restrictive monetary policy would harm economic performance. Hence, as long as inflation is under control, slightly higher rates are acceptable. Moreover, it should be analyzed what factors cause inflation. If it is tightening in the labor market, then policy intervention can be withdrawn at least partially because its objective of full employment is achieved. If inflation is caused by the economy running beyond its actual capacity, economic policy may be more strongly targeted to capacity-enhancing investment.

Intervening economic policy is not able to achieve economic objectives with precision. There are many unforeseeable occurrences while policy impacts only materialize with a delay. Moreover, weak institutions in developing countries may provide little expert capacity for the targeted investment sectors. Likewise, administrative resources for execution are often insufficient. We thus could come back to the need for good institutions as a precondition for economic prosperity. While this does not necessarily mean institutions, which merely focus on property rights and competitive markets, it is obviously a truism that good institutions facilitate development. However, the building of institutions also requires extensive resources such as skilled labor, training and collective administrative experience.

Institutions may support growth but they are themselves not value-creating. It is therefore a doubtful strategy to start with investing development countries' very scarce resources in the improvement of institutions. This is why economic development and higher incomes are required first to create those resources. More than institutions being a precondition for growth, growth is a precondition for better institutions.[5] Taking institutions as what they are, developing countries should use them to implement active economic policy programs as described here to raise living standards. Out of this, resources are generated to stepwise improve institutions.

Going back to the scenery of a street market in a developing country, what would the basic principles of such policy intervention be? The government could target a specific sector to be developed. This could be investment in agriculture or the development of a domestic textile industry instead of importing second-hand clothes. This is what, for example, Ethiopia, Ruanda and other East and Central African countries are aiming at (see de Freytas-Tamura 2018). It involves a lot of planning as also energy supply and transport systems are required and therefore, it is a big policy and economic challenge for poor countries. However, this reveals even

---

[5]For a critical assessment of the role of institutions in economic development, see Chang (2011).

more clearly that the market is not able to fulfill these tasks. It is only production that creates value. Hence, only production generates more goods as well as the additional income to be spent on those goods.

References

Arestis P, Sawyer M (2003) Reinventing fiscal policy. J Post Keynesian Econ 26(1):3–25
Chang H-J (2011) Institutions and economic development: theory, policy and history. J Institut Econ 7(4):473–498. https://doi.org/10.1017/S1744137410000378
de Freytas-Tamura K (2018) Auch eine Frage der Würde. Le monde diplomatique, February 2018. https://monde-diplomatique.de/artikel/!5480549. Accessed 4 Feb 2020
UNCTAD (2014) World investment report 2014. Investing in the SDGs: an Action Plan. https://unctad.org/system/files/official-document/wir2014_en.pdf. Accessed 7 Feb 2020
Wray LR (2015) Modern money theory: a primer on macroeconomics for sovereign monetary systems, 2nd edn. Palgrave Macmillan, New York

Chapter 6
Developing Countries in Global Capitalism

So far, we have considered macroeconomic principles in general as well as applied to developing countries. Thereby, only the internal macroeconomic structure of those countries has played a role. However, in reality developing countries do not operate in an isolated space. They are embedded in the world economy. This makes economic dynamics more complex. In today's globalized capitalism, the scope of action for developing countries is strongly restricted. Let us look at the reasons for this.

6.1 International Trade and Financial Flows

A national economy maintains trade relationships with other countries. As part of this, exports and imports do not necessarily have to balance. This has several implications. For a monetary circuit to be started and closed, it needs a banking system including a central bank, which is able to issue monetary units. Different banking systems issue money in different currencies. It is therefore easy to understand that every currency area creates its own monetary circuit. Most currency areas are identical with individual countries but some may extend over a group of countries such as the Euro zone or the Franc zones in West and Central Africa. Regardless, the circuit is the bottom line of the monetary economy of production. International trade implies that goods are exchanged between different production economies and, hence, circuits. With regard to exports, a part of the demand for domestic goods comes from abroad. On the other hand, when goods are imported a part of the demand created by the domestic economy goes abroad.

Let us take the perspective of a single small developing country trading with the rest of the world. International trade is settled in a global key currency, most often the US dollar. To understand international economic relations, we have to know what determines the exchange rate between currencies, that is, their relative prices.

As already introduced at the beginning, neoclassical theory relies on Ricardo's theory of comparative advantage. The so-called purchasing power parity (PPP) model argues that when a country has a trade deficit, it has to purchase foreign currency to pay for it. This makes foreign currency scarcer relative to the country's own currency such that the latter's relative price falls. This currency depreciation means that the country's exports become cheaper in the rest of the world because goods prices measured in domestic currency now are lower when calculated in foreign currency. Meanwhile, imports become more expensive to purchase because whereas foreign goods still have the same prices in foreign currency, they increase in terms of domestic currency. Thanks to the depreciation, the deficit country becomes competitive and can lower its imports and raise its exports. It improves its trade balance until it is equilibrated again. The opposite happens in the case of an initial trade surplus: the currency appreciates such that it becomes harder to sell exports while there is an incentive to raise imports as they have become cheaper. Free trade thus is self-regulating.

The PPP model can be complemented by the famous Dornbusch model, which also includes financial flows (Dornbusch 1976). Differences in money supply across countries give way to different interest rates. Countries with expansive monetary policy and strongly growing money supply have lower interest rates than those with restrictive policy. In a comparison between two countries, the high-rate country is more attractive for financial investment. Demand for its currency thus tends to increase and appreciate it. However, it does not come as a surprise that even this model ends up in an equilibrium. This means that there has to be an equilibrium of relative prices in the goods market as well as an equilibrium of interest rates in the financial market. The mechanism can briefly be summed up as follows: the exchange rate changes such that it first establishes the equilibrium of interest rates. With some delay, relative price levels also adjust such that the balanced-trade equilibrium is also established in the goods market. Since prices increase again more in the country with the higher money supply and the lower interest rate relative to prices in the other country, money supply relative to the price level eventually is again equal as initially such that interest rates are equalized, too.

Instead of going more into the technical details of these models, let us go to the core of relevance with regard to our analysis. These mainstream explanations of the exchange rate, as common as they may seem, are based on mistaken assumptions. First of all, why would the price of a currency go up when demand for it increases? This would be the case if money was a scarce commodity. But it is not. Money is tied to credit creation. So any demand for currency can basically be satisfied by the banking system issuing that currency at no cost. Therefore, the exchange rate does not necessarily have to change.

Second, changes in exports and imports may be due to different growth rates across countries. For instance, higher growth in one country usually leads to an increase in imports because people can afford more consumption. Therefore, trade flows are not only determined by relative prices between countries but also, and probably even more, by the whole set of macroeconomic dynamics. Additionally, the non-linear relationship between monetary policy and inflation has been

Table 6.1 The composition of the current account

	Exports of goods and services
−	Imports of goods and services
=	**Trade balance**
+	Returns from investments abroad earned by domestic residents
−	Returns of foreign investments earned by foreign residents
+	Net transfers (remittances, social transfers)
=	**Current account**

explained. We know that a change in the money supply that is supposed to alter interest rates will not simply lead to a proportional increase of price levels, which brings all variables back to equilibrium in a miraculous way.

We now want to find a better explanation of exchange rate movements. Let us start with the nominal exchange rate, that is, the relative value of currencies, and then have a look at the real exchange rate. The analysis of nominal exchange rate determination has been strongly brought forward by post-Keynesian economics as well as the school of thought called quantum macroeconomics (Cencini and Schmitt 1991).

If there is a trade surplus, the country receives more foreign currency from its exports than it has to pay for its imports. It accumulates currency reserves. In case of a trade deficit, the country can either draw on reserves stemming from past surpluses or it has to access a loan in foreign currency. In this case, the country gets indebted towards the rest of the world. It will have to run a surplus in the future to earn the currency again for debt repayment. Yet, the trade balance is not the only factor determining the need for foreign currency. There is income of domestic residents earned abroad as well as income of people abroad earned in the domestic economy. These are mostly capital returns from investments. Interest that is earned on foreign reserves or has to be paid on foreign debt is included here. Specifically, for developing countries, there are also social transfers from development cooperation and remittances sent from emigrants to their families. In total, there results a net sum of earnings from trade and other financial flows called the current account. The current account determines the total need for foreign currency. This is summarized in the following simplified hierarchy of accounting positions in Table 6.1.

The so-called capital account is the 'back side' of the current account. It defines its financial side, that is, how foreign currency is provided. It may, for example, come from direct foreign investment, that is, investment of foreign residents in real assets in the domestic economy. On the other hand, when domestic residents invest abroad, capital flows out of the country. While foreign direct investment usually is oriented towards the long term, financial flows may also be quite short-term and speculative. As will be discussed, they may reverse and flow out as fast as they have flown in. To the extent that inflows of foreign capital are insufficient to cover a current account deficit, the country has to access a foreign loan. In the opposite case, abundant capital inflows add to the central bank's holdings of reserve currency.

Table 6.2 Example of a developing country's balance of payments

Current account		Capital account	
Net exports of goods and services	< 0	Foreign direct investment	> 0
Net income from cross-border investments	< 0	Net portfolio flows	> 0
Remittances	> 0	Increase in net foreign debt	> 0
Foreign aid	> 0		
Change in official reserves	≈ 0		
Total	X	Total	X

The sum of the current account and the capital account is the balance of payments. As a matter of logic, the balance of payments is always 'balanced' because the current account and the capital account are of the same size. When a country has a positive current account, that is, it earns more from abroad than the rest of the world earns from the country, net holdings of foreign currency increase meaning that the surplus is invested abroad. In the opposite case, there is a net outflow of currency, which has to be covered by financial inflows via debt. Therefore, the balance of payments is actually neither an equation nor an equilibrium or disequilibrium but an identity.

Basically, whenever a country needs access to foreign currency to cover a current account deficit, a loan can be provided by a foreign bank. Since money supply is infinitely elastic, there is no scarcity in foreign currency. Hence, there is no reason to argue that relative prices of currencies change. This is why accessing such an external loan does not cause a change in the exchange rate. Likewise, when net exports yield reserves of foreign currency, exporters are provided with newly created domestic money on their deposits in exchange for the foreign currency, which is held as reserves in the banking system. Money creation immediately satisfies increased demand for domestic currency so that there is no appreciation of the home currency against foreign currency. Current account and capital account describe the two sides of the same item.

To make the subject of the balance of payments better understandable, the following simplified representation in Table 6.2 shows a typical balance of payments of a developing country in a certain year.[1] It is likely that the country features a trade deficit and also is a net debtor such that there are net outflows of cross-border capital incomes. On the other hand, remittances and foreign aid flows are most often positive. In a period of macroeconomic stability, it is also justified to assume, on average, a net inflow of foreign direct investment and portfolio investment. However, to the extent that this is not sufficient to cover a suggested external deficit, the country has to incur new foreign debt, which thus adds to the existing stock of debt. When capital inflows and the increase in debt are above what is needed to pay for the current account deficit, the extra currency adds to the official reserves. However, in a

---

[1] It may be helpful to note that the term 'balance' is not really appropriate in macroeconomic accounting of international financial and real flows. Balances usually define stocks in a certain point in time while the balance of payments involves flows over a specific time period.

situation like the one described here, a constant increase in reserves is unlikely while a constant decrease is not affordable.

6.2 Explanation of Exchange Rate Fluctuations

But then, where do exchange rate fluctuations come from? This point is not obvious and often goes unnoticed. In today's international monetary system, international payments are different from payments within a national economy. Take the case where a person abroad wants to make a payment to another person in a specific country with a different currency. While the payment is made in a global key currency, mostly US dollars, the payee receives it in domestic currency. This works as follows: in general, a payment means that the ownership over a bank deposit changes from the payer to the payee. For international payments like in our example, the deposit in US dollars offered by the payer is not directly received by the payee. In fact, the payee's bank receives the dollar deposit and simultaneously adds the corresponding amount in domestic currency to the deposit of the payee. As a result, the bank's balance sheet grows. On its asset side, there is the newly registered deposit in US dollars. However, this does not mean that the bank gets a free lunch. The dollar deposit is matched by the increased deposit of the payee on the liability side of the bank's balance sheet.

Important to understand, this new deposit in domestic currency is newly created money. At the same time, the size of the balance sheet of the foreign bank from where the payment is made remains the same. It does not shrink because the deposit in US dollars still exists as an entry in the foreign bank, the only difference being that ownership of that deposit has changed. The sum of both balance sheets thus grows. Overall, there is thus an increase in monetary units, which the receiving bank enters as deposit in domestic currency in its balance sheet.[2] In a more detailed analysis, we would have to not only speak about individual banks but about the respective national banking systems since currency reserves that are received by a country enter the central bank's balance sheet. Yet, without loss of generality we assume that the banking systems each consist of a single bank.

We see that an international payment changes the amount of money in the country of the non-key currency. An additional payment in the opposite direction to the one described above involves the same mechanism. The payer pays with domestic currency while the bank can use its foreign currency deposit to make the payment to the payees' deposit abroad. The bank's balance sheet shrinks again. Alternatively, or if there are no more reserves, the bank has to approach a loan in foreign currency

---

[2] This means that the deposits are doubled because the foreign currency deposit is now registered in the domestic bank's balance sheet while also remaining as an entry in the foreign bank. This mechanism of 'monetary duplication' was first emphasized by Jacques Rueff (1963). For details, see Cencini (2000).

to make the payment on behalf of its depositor. In this case, it is the balance sheet of the payee's bank in the other country, which grows. The case of the deficit country will be considered in more detail. It is not very likely that a banking system uses its reserves systematically to make payments for commercial imports. Reserves are rather used to meet other purposes than trade as is to be seen. So, trade deficits are usually paid by referring to foreign loans to the extent required.

The new deposits created in the course of international payments are treated as if they were not only monetary units but assets. As such, they can be traded. This happens on the foreign exchange market where commercial banks and central banks are the main traders. Additionally, there are large multinational corporations and also large hedge funds. When it is said that currencies are traded, in fact, it is trade with bank deposits that are denominated in different currencies (whether aware of this fact or not). While true money is not scarce and therefore cannot have the character of a distinct asset, things are different with these deposits.[3] Exchanging deposits denominated in different currencies implies that they have a price expressed in the respective other currency. This relative price changes according to supply and demand in the foreign exchange market. Hence the fluctuations in the exchange rate.

Why is this explanation of exchange rate determination different from the more familiar one given by mainstream economics? First of all, the exchange rate does not automatically change when there is a trade surplus or deficit. Even though there may be an indirect connection as we will see, we have established the result that the nature of money as being created by the banking system provides the option of stable currency values independent of trade patterns. Second, the exchange rate as being determined by supply of and demand for currency in the foreign exchange market is subject to various influences, which can involve rather uncertain patterns of the exchange rate.

There are several central factors that have an influence on the value of a currency whereas with value in this context we mean the price of a currency expressed in another currency. One of these factors is international payments for interest. External debt involves interest that is also due in foreign currency. For this, the debtor bank (or banking system, respectively) has to offer domestic currency against foreign currency in the foreign exchange market, if it does not want to finance interest payments via further increasing foreign debt.[4] This means that, at a given exchange rate, there is excess supply of the domestic currency relative to the foreign currency. As a result, the domestic currency tends to depreciate. The mechanics of foreign debt servicing also implies that trade imbalances actually can have an impact on the exchange rate. The higher the trade deficit, the higher the current account deficit and hence external debt tends to be. Consequently, a larger trade deficit tends to go along

---

[3] In detail: from the principle of the monetary circuit, we know that money is associated with output. However, international payments give rise to the creation of new deposits to which no output corresponds. This is why currency reserves are created, which can be traded as assets.

[4] This is where the payment for debt services is different from those in international trade. In the latter, the foreign exchange market is not involved as long as trade deficits are covered by foreign loans.

with a higher burden of interest on foreign debt, thus putting depreciating pressure on the exchange rate.

As a second factor, profit expectations influence the attractiveness of a currency. The higher the interest rate level in a country, the higher the return that can be earned on a bank deposit or on bonds. The same argument concerns the profitability in the economy or, respectively, overall economic performance. If the profit rate in an economy is considered as above average, demand for currency of that economy increases as it can be productively invested in the country. The currencies of those economies with relatively high interest rates or profit rates tend to appreciate because demand for them in the foreign exchange market increases.

Yet, the joint impact of these two variables on the exchange rate may not be straightforward because the relationship between the interest rate and the profit rate is complex and likely to change over time. On the one hand, a high profit rate can afford a higher interest rate without being compromised too much. On the other hand, low interest rates may push up the profit rate because they may accelerate investment. This is particularly the case when low interest rates trigger speculative investment in financial markets as capital is searching for alternative sources of profit. Rising prices of financial assets yield extra profits at least for a certain time period. In this scenario, profit expectations are low with respect to interest on bank deposits or bonds but high regarding profits from production or speculation. The final impact on the exchange rate might remain ambiguous.

Third, there are also speculative transactions in the foreign exchange market. There may be trade of currencies to benefit from exchange rate changes while itself triggering exchange rate volatility. As part of this, capital flight also has an impact on the exchange rate. It can take different channels. Wealth owners want to bring their wealth out of the country by purchasing foreign currency, thus involving an exchange rate depreciation. They may suddenly grow to uncontrollable size such that central banks have to intervene to defend exchange rate stability by releasing currency reserves in the foreign exchange market. Once reserves become tight, the monetary authorities are forced to let the currency depreciate.

Capital flight is a complex phenomenon. It can take legal ways through ordinary international payments as well as illegal transactions. The motivation behind it is usually that wealth owners consider their wealth as threatened. Reasons often are policy influence such as higher taxes, development strategies involving active state intervention in the market, or expropriation. The outflow of financial wealth means that the respective country is deprived of resources, which cannot be employed in productive activity anymore. Capital flight may also be triggered by the fear of wealth devaluation due to inflation or exchange rate depreciation. In response to an initial devaluation, capital flight therefore may increase further because fear of continuing wealth devaluation makes investors and wealth owners look for a 'safe haven'. Thereby, it triggers a self-enforcing process of depreciation.

Obviously, the opposite of capital flight can also happen. Waves of capital inflows via the foreign exchange market tend to appreciate the currency. The mechanism is the one described in the stylized setting of the two countries and the two banks above. Foreign wealth owners want to move their money, and thus literally their bank deposit in foreign currency, to their country of interest. This means that the bank of that country receives a payment in foreign currency, which adds to the official reserves. The foreign wealth owner is provided with a new deposit of the corresponding amount of money in domestic currency at the domestic bank of the new country. Again, we observe an increase of the amount of money available in the economy. Foreign investors may purchase real and financial assets in the domestic economy and thereby contribute to the build-up of financial bubbles.

In the same vein, in times of strong capital inflows demand for the respective national currency increases in the foreign exchange market. The central bank could accommodate this demand by providing all the money in national currency in order to ensure a stable exchange rate. This would prevent an appreciation, which may be considered as harmful for the domestic economy and its export sector. Yet, exchange rate stability implies that more monetary units are created in response to the capital inflows compared to the case where an appreciation is allowed for.

These explanations just give a glimpse of the dynamics in the foreign exchange market. But they are sufficient to see that the determination of the nominal exchange rate is quite complex. The different driving factors change in weight and direction. There is a lot of uncertainty since speculation in the foreign exchange market is also influenced by agents' expectations of how the exchange rate will effectively turn out, which again affects its volatility.

6.3   No Trade Equilibrium Guaranteed

Finally, international trade flows are not determined by the nominal exchange rate but by the real exchange rate. That is, we have to add prices to the nominal exchange rate. Considering the nominal rate as given for a moment, exports are the more competitive, the lower their price compared to prices in the rest of the world. This means that if the domestic currency depreciates, it does not gain a competitive advantage for its exports if prices of those exports increase by the same amount. This would be a zero-sum game in terms of relative prices. As another example, if the nominal exchange rate remains stable but the rest of the world features a higher inflation rate, and hence a higher price level than the domestic economy, the latter gains a competitive advantage.

In neoclassical theory, nominal exchange rate and price levels complement each other. If there is inflation as triggered by too high a money supply in the domestic economy, the nominal exchange rate depreciates such that the initial equilibrium is restored. If the nominal exchange rate is flexible, it adjusts to changing relative prices. If it is fixed (for reasons to be explained), relative prices do the job of adjustment. In each case, we end up with an equilibrium exchange rate, which goes along with balanced trade as explained in the PPP model.

A more realistic view is a less harmonic one. For now, let us take the nominal exchange rate as given. To understand how we get from the nominal to the real exchange rate, the classical analysis is helpful.[5] Goods prices consist of production costs and profits. Production costs divide into wages and material inputs. The latter is again produced by workers and possibly other material inputs. Hence, eventually production costs are a composition of wages. Labor produces at a certain level of productivity. The higher the productivity, the lower unit costs and the lower prices. Hence, higher productivity allows for higher wages without driving production costs upward.

Based on Marx' (1894/2004, p. 180) insight, profit rates tend to equalize across sectors as well as internationally. From there, it follows that prices are linked to production costs. When production costs increase, goods prices go up more or less proportionally because profits are added proportionally everywhere. For this reason, we can say that relative price levels of two countries are determined by their relative production costs. The country with lower production costs has a competitive advantage.

This finding has important consequences. Since a competitive advantage is due to lower production costs, it means that this advantage is absolute instead of only comparative in the sense that it does not help if countries specialize in a certain sector so that everyone is better off. The country with lower production costs tends to run a trade surplus in all sectors towards the country with higher production costs. The latter thus faces a deficit rather than self-rebalancing trade. Ricardo's theory is not of much help here.

To see the difference between the mainstream and the classical explanation of exchange rates as presented here, let us assume that our considered country has higher production costs than its trading partner. In the mainstream explanation, the currency would simply devalue until production costs are equal, which gives way to balanced trade. However, a depreciating currency would mean that imports get more expensive such that workers in the domestic economy can only buy fewer goods. The effect of this is that their wages have fallen not in nominal terms but in real terms. Wages are the same in monetary units but their purchasing power has declined due to more expensive imports. Lower wages imply that real production costs have gone down, too. Therefore, workers bargain for higher wages in order to restore their purchasing power. Once the latter is regained, production costs are back to the same level. Relative prices are what they were initially. By contrast, if purchasing power cannot be reclaimed, the competitive advantage remains.

Differences in production costs can persist for an undefined time. There is no equilibrating mechanism that would automatically lead to balanced trade. Trade deficits and surpluses are likely to sustain for long as for instance the persisting US current account deficit since the 1970s shows. Changes in the nominal exchange rate only impact on the real exchange rate to the extent that they change relative

---

[5]See Shaikh (2016) who made crucial contributions to the understanding of the determination of real exchange rates.

production costs. In the above example, this would mean that after a currency depreciation, workers reclaim only a part but not everything of their initial purchasing power.

6.4   Trying to Control the Exchange Rate

Neither the nominal nor the real exchange rate is driven by mechanisms that would automatically entail stability and trade balance equilibrium. Instead, their determination is driven by various forces the relative influence of which is uncertain and subject to changes over time. Yet, what is the problem about fluctuations in the exchange rate? There are many.

As mentioned, an exchange rate depreciation involves higher import prices when translated into domestic currency. Via material inputs to production, they feed through to the domestic price level. Inflation has the well-known effects that it involves instability and hampered efficiency in resource allocation due to biased price signals. Inflationary effects of currency devaluation can be quite strong. They increase uncertainty for investors and thereby may induce further depreciation caused by investment relocation. Moreover, in the case the devaluation was an official objective in order to achieve an improvement in international competitiveness, inflation nullifies the gains at least partially such that pressure to further devalue the currency may increase. We see again that an exchange rate depreciation can be self-enforcing.

Moreover, a weaker currency implies that external debt weighs heavier. More money in domestic currency needs to be earned and exchanged against foreign currency to repay the same amount of debt. This is an existential problem for all debtors who owe money in foreign currency. Notably, banks can get into serious problems if their assets are denominated in domestic currency while liabilities are due in foreign currency. For the economy, a devaluated currency means that more goods have to be exported in the future to pay back external debt. Externally indebted banks and firms may contract investment activities and retain profits in order to deleverage their balance sheets. Both effects hamper demand and the overall economy. This is particularly relevant for developing countries because they rely more on finance in foreign currency than advanced economies who are better able to borrow in their own currency due to the strength of their economies and currencies as perceived by investors.

If an exchange rate depreciation is caused by capital flight, it can easily be that the process of devaluation gets out of control because the self-enforcing tendency is quite strong. Exchange rate depreciation can therefore give rise to a banking crisis because the heavier burden of foreign debt may mean bankruptcy for banks. And it can end up in a currency crisis where continued devaluation of the domestic currency, if it comes to the worst, means hyperinflation and the breakdown of economic activity. Banking and currency crises often go hand in hand.

The opposite case of an exchange rate appreciation has the opposite conse-quences. Import prices fall so that production costs decrease. At the same time, there is downward pressure on export prices in order to not lose competitiveness in the world market. Resulting deflation means that economic agents postpone expen-ditures as they expect them to become cheaper in the future. The corresponding drop in effective demand weakens economic dynamics and possibly even leads to con-traction. An advantage can be that foreign debt becomes lighter to carry. In the opposite scenario, to the extent that the country enjoyed currency account surpluses in the past, exchange rate appreciation also means the devaluation of accumulated foreign reserves.

The best-known argument in favor of an exchange rate depreciation is the gain of a competitive advantage allowing to turn the trade deficit into a surplus. The strategy can be successful. Yet, apart from the possible real revaluation due to accelerating inflation, success depends on the so-called Marshall-Lerner condition (see Blecker and Setterfield 2019, pp. 468–470). It says that the expansion of net exports in response to an exchange rate depreciation is strong enough to bring about an improvement in the trade balance. A currency devaluation tends to increase the volume of exports and lower that of imports. This is the quantity effect. However, the quantities are priced differently now. The same export good is cheaper to buy abroad, which implies that it yields less return measured in foreign currency. On the other hand, an imported good becomes more expensive in domestic currency. These two impacts describe the price effect. Thus, a depreciation only improves the trade balance if the quantity effect is stronger than the price effect. For an exchange rate depreciation to be effective, the impact of increased export quantities and reduced import quantities must not be nullified by altered export and import prices.

After all, both a currency depreciation as well as an appreciation may have some advantages. However, they also involve serious problems. A change in the exchange rate may be appropriate under certain circumstances. But to ensure economic stability, it has to take place in a controlled way, which is hardly the case with the mechanisms at work in today's determination of exchange rates.

The wish to control the exchange rate has led countries to introduce pegs. A pegged exchange rate means that the central bank sets a target of the rate between the domestic and a selected global or regional key currency. In principle, a peg can also involve a basket of weighted foreign currencies that is targeted. To realize this target, the central bank intervenes in the foreign exchange market. When the domestic currency tends to be too weak compared to the anchor currency, it releases foreign currency out of its reserves and uses it to purchase domestic currency. This increases demand for the domestic currency in the foreign exchange market while making foreign currency more abundant. If the currency is appreciating above the peg target, additional reserves are purchased while at the same time creating new deposits in domestic currency. This measure makes foreign currency in the foreign exchange market scarcer while increasing the availability of national currency.

There is an extensive debate on whether a free-floating or a pegged exchange rate system is better.[6] The latter has some obvious advantages: it helps keep inflation low because exchange rate volatility as an important source of inflation is ruled out. Macroeconomic stability increases. On the other hand, in the pegged system, the central bank should set the interest rate at an appropriate level relative to that in the country of the anchor country. Too high a difference between the interest rates would trigger capital flows between the countries, thereby triggering exchange rate volatility. The monetary authority has to put more effort into guaranteeing exchange rate stability via intervention in the foreign exchange market. Hence, exchange rate pegging implies that the respective country loses autonomy in monetary policy. The central bank is not free anymore to set the interest rate such that it best serves the needs of the domestic economy. Additionally, if inflation in the anchor country increases, it spills over to the country with the pegged exchange rate. The country then has to accept higher inflation and cannot act against it by, for example, increasing the interest rate or gradually appreciating the currency.

Furthermore, it is questionable if a country's currency reserves are sufficient to defend an exchange rate target, especially when there is accelerating capital flight or speculative attacks to provoke depreciation. In case the central bank has to give up the target, the corresponding devaluation shock might be much larger than if a freely floating exchange rate had allowed for a gradual adjustment. Likewise, investors may even anticipate the introduction of an exchange rate peg and therefore already transfer capital in advance. The introduction and abolition of pegging is thus tied to specific risks. This is especially true for developing countries, which usually have quite limited capacity to defend an exchange rate target.

If financial flows in the foreign exchange market exert upward rather than downward pressure on the exchange rate, it is easier to defend the exchange rate target. All the central bank has to do is to purchase foreign reserves in order to lower relative demand for the domestic currency. However, as we have explained, such purchases involve the payments that lead to an increase in the amount of money because in exchange for foreign reserves, the central bank provides the currency seller with a new deposit in domestic currency. This new money may be used by investors to exert additional demand for real and financial assets, thereby creating bubbles. Exchange rate pegging thus can also contribute to additional instability. Apart from the fluctuations in the exchange rate, capital inflows can be as much a problem for macroeconomic stability as capital outflows.

It is, however, an illusion to believe that free-floating exchange rates allow for a completely autonomous monetary policy that can be tailor-fitted to the domestic economy. Even countries with flexible exchange rates can afford neither unlimited depreciations nor appreciations. This means that they have to set interest rates such that exchange rate stability is broadly ensured. Indeed, in the middle to long term central bank interest rates in different countries all over the world reveal significant

---

[6]For an overview of the arguments in favor of and against exchange rate pegging (though not neutral), see Mishkin (1998).

correlation implying that they move more or less in the same direction (Mohanty 2014). The monetary authority may not intervene in the foreign exchange market to realize an official target. But exchange rate stability is usually at least unofficially an issue of great importance. Interest rate policy takes this fact into account and then meets the dilemma that it cannot serve two goals, that is, exchange rate stability and domestic economic performance, at the same time. This dilemma is just as well-known to central banks in a flexible regime as to those in a pegged one.

Moreover, a central bank may be convinced to let the exchange rate float as long as global and national macroeconomic conditions are stable anyway. In more turbulent times of crises, such a conduct of policy might be complemented by foreign exchange market intervention rather soon. Therefore, in reality both stances on how to deal with exchange rates are more similar than it seems at first sight. This is simply due to the fact that both approaches use the same limited number of instruments to deal with the problems brought about by exchange rate fluctuations.

Box 6.1 The Vulnerability of Open Economies: The Asian Crisis

The Asian crisis of 1997 may be the best showcase of how countries are limited on their development path by international economic dynamics. The crisis hit Thailand, Indonesia and South Korea most but Malaysia, Singapore, the Philippines, Taiwan, and Hong Kong were affected, too. As an additional effect, the liquidity crunch produced global repercussions, mainly via a drop in stock prices in the United States and a slowdown in economic growth in Japan. The internal economic situation differed between those South East Asian countries but also revealed many common features.

The countries enjoyed high growth rates, which were fueled by inflows of foreign capital. Believing in high returns, foreign investors did not worry about the countries' current account deficits, which they kept financing. In fact, however, a lot of foreign capital was feeding speculative bubbles in these countries. Foreign debt grew but this could not go on forever. In the early 1990s, the US started to increase interest rates. Consequently, international financial flows turned more and more to the US where interest returns were higher. This gave way to the appreciation of the US dollar. For the South East Asian countries, it became harder to keep their currencies pegged to the US dollar, which was the monetary policy objective at that time. Additionally, capital flight and speculative attacks against their currencies eventually enforced their devaluation. Starting with the depreciation of the Thai baht, financial capital waves forced one central bank after the other to give up the exchange rate target.

Devaluation of the countries' currencies entailed initial defaults in the private sector on foreign loans. They were enough to trigger a decrease in asset prices, which subsequently led to their collapse. Needless to say, the banking crisis in combination with the currency crisis triggered even more

---

(continued)

Box 6.1 (continued)

capital flight, hence enforcing further exchange rate depreciations. Central banks tried to maintain their currency's value by selling foreign currency reserves. Moreover, they raised interest rates in order to reduce the spread to the rates of other countries such as the US. The IMF provided support in the form of additional loans to endow the countries with foreign reserves. Yet, all these measures could not prevent the collapse of the currencies.

The IMF's loans did not come unconditional but with structural adjustment. Governments were forced to reduce spending and to increase interest rates in order to ensure a stable exchange rate as the first condition. Ironically, during the decades before the crisis, it was the IMF who had recommended the elimination of capital controls in order to liberalize global financial flows. By contrast, China was less affected by the Asian crisis because it had not liberalized its financial account. The Chinese renminbi still cannot be traded freely internationally, which makes it much easier to control the exchange rate.

The experience of the Asian crisis strengthened the criticism of the Washington consensus as it was clearly seen that financial liberalization involves very high macroeconomic risks. Another consequence was that lending to developing countries was considered as riskier. For developing and emerging economies, the risk of current account deficits and the related fragility became major issues of concern. Many of them pursued a restructuring of their economic sectors in order to run current account surpluses. Hence, export-led growth appeared as the safe way out of instability. Many of the emerging Asian countries followed this path, also allowing them the accumulation of foreign reserves to be used in times of financial stress (Eichengreen 2011, pp. 114–115). While the Asian crisis reveals the problem of external deficits in the course of economic growth, we also know that export-driven development has its own weaknesses and has contributed to today's global imbalances in trade and financial flows.

6.5 Capital Controls as Part of the Solution

These are some of the arguments in favor and against exchange rate pegging. The perfect system does not seem to exist. This is why capital controls are debated as an additional instrument and a possible way out of the dilemma. The term of capital controls covers measures, which aim to control, and usually limit, the size and types of capital flows in and out of the economy.

Capital controls can take different forms such as the prohibition of certain investment vehicles and sectors for foreign investors, minimum stay periods for capital in domestic deposits before it can be transferred abroad again, or taxation of international transactions to make them unattractive. When there are barriers to certain transactions, speculative investments, which aim at benefiting from quite small exchange rate variations, can be reduced. Moreover, short-termed capital flows rely on the option of withdrawing investment fast. Capital controls may prevent this and thus not only reduce capital outflows but also inflows. With fewer transactions, the exchange rate is less exposed to volatility.

It comes as no surprise that capital controls are barely supported by mainstream economics (see for example Rogoff 2002) even though nowadays there are several economists favoring them even there. The general equilibrium approach is based on the assumption that the market yields the best outcome to maximize utility of individuals. According to this view, capital controls prevent the transactions needed to realize the efficient equilibrium. Anything that hampers capital mobility inevitably distorts the market. Moreover, to the extent that capital controls prevent a depreciation or appreciation of the currency one could even say that they distort the beneficial efficiency of international trade because the exchange rate cannot find the level required for balanced trade.

It is also argued that trade liberalization and financial liberalization have to go hand in hand. If goods are to move flexibly without trade barriers, finance should be allowed to do likewise. Trade requires payments and hence a corresponding flow of finance. Therefore, the latter has to be liberalized so that the former can be conducted as foreseen by the theory of free trade. However, we have shown that there is no inherent tendency of trade to equilibrate. Moreover, financial flows involve exchange rate volatility as well as macroeconomic and financial instability. Hence, there is a strong case to apply capital controls. Once exchange rate fluctuations are reduced by this additional instrument, the central bank has more scope of action to use the conventional instrument of interest rate targeting again to meet the needs of the domestic economy.

Yet, there are certain critical points about capital controls. They can be circumvented because it is not always easy to distinguish types of capital flows such that the measures are not always effective in preventing the targeted ones. It is true that trade requires the corresponding financial flows to be finally settled. To the extent that a country runs a current account deficit, capital inflows are necessary. Some of the inflows such as foreign direct investment are oriented towards the long term. In order to only prevent unnecessary speculative and short-term flows but not those related to trade and productive investment, capital controls cannot be too strict, which provides space for circumvention. On the other hand, payments can be disguised as being made for import or export of goods even though the actual aim is the shift of capital.

Moreover, shadow markets may emerge where currencies are exchanged in cash. Exchange rates in these shadow markets tend to be quite different from the official rates. The latter can be kept within a certain margin thanks to capital controls, which limit or exclude certain agents from participation in the trade of currencies. The unofficial rate in the shadow market, by contrast, materializes at a different level since at least a part of the officially blocked financial flows finds its way to the marketplace, though an illegal one. Capital controls thus require a lot of administrative skills and may create bureaucratic processes. In many developing countries, these processes are complicated but sometimes ineffective and provide another source of corruption.

In the same vein as the fixing of the exchange rate, capital controls face challenges when they are to be implemented and abandoned. Anticipating the introduction of capital controls, investors and speculators may even intensify transactions as long as they are unregulated. This is particularly relevant for the case of capital flight. After an exit from controls, capital flows may take off and those transactions that were prevented before now take place all at once.

And, very basically, capital controls reduce some of the sources of exchange rate fluctuations such as speculative capital flows. However, they cannot influence trade imbalances, external indebtedness and payments of foreign interest, which all contribute to exchange rate changes. Even with capital controls, the mechanism of international payments entailing the creation of new monetary units, which then are traded as currencies in the foreign exchange market, remains in place. The role of capital controls should not be minimized as they have their merits in developing and emerging countries' management of financial flows. But capital controls alone cannot guarantee exchange rate stability.

6.6 The Balance-of-Payments Restriction

Now that we have opened the economy to the rest of the world in our analysis, many more complexities are involved. It is not only relevant what happens in the domestic economy but also what domestic economic development means for its relations to the rest of the world. Individuals, companies or even the public sector cannot accumulate unlimited debt. At some point, debt may become unbearable and the debtor's creditworthiness declines, expressing itself in higher risk premia on interest rates.

The same is true for the economy as a whole. Too high deficits in the current account, and thus notably in international trade, involve a currency devaluation via the foreign exchange market. Exchange rate depreciation, as we have seen, entails inflation, heavier burden of foreign debt, and can give rise to a banking crisis. The stronger the effect, the more economic activity is damaged. Moreover, to repay foreign debt, a higher share of domestic production needs to be exported in the future so that the foreign currency for debt service can be earned.

Exchange rate depreciation, and uncontrolled exchange rate volatility in general, hampers any development strategy. Through economic contraction and revaluation of foreign liabilities, the country is deprived of resources, which are so essential to foster economic growth and improve living standards. For poverty reduction to be successfully achieved in a country, the balance of payments must be balanced at least in the middle to long term. Exchange rate pegging and capital controls can, in some situations support stability, but their power is limited.

Why are we discussing exchange rates and the factors influencing them in such detail? Here we are at a point of such tremendous importance that any macroeconomic strategy for developing countries that neglects its implications is doomed to failure. The balance of payments equilibrium is the trade balance that includes an equilibrated current account meaning that cross-border flows of incomes are balanced. An equilibrated balance of payments entails a restriction for economic growth and development.

Economic growth means higher incomes that are divided into purchases in the domestic market and imports from abroad. As long as these respective shares do not change dramatically, rising income goes along with growing imports. This deteriorates the trade balance and contributes to a current account deficit. Increasing imports could be compensated by enhanced exports. However, the latter do not grow equally when income in the country increases. Instead, exports depend on demand from abroad and therefore economic growth and income in the rest of the world. Most countries are far too small to influence performance of the world economy. For a single developing country, economic growth in other countries is just a given fact. From this, it can easily be concluded that when a country increases economic growth, its imports increase while exports do not alter, thus giving way to a deterioration in the trade balance.

The higher the growth of an economy compared to the rest of the world, the larger the current account deficit. Economic stability and long-term prosperity require a balance of payments equilibrium in order to prevent disturbances in exchange rate. Moreover, foreign debt needs to be kept at controllable amounts. Due to this long-term requirement of external balance, there is a maximum rate at which the economy is allowed to grow. This condition is known as the balance of payments constraint, the external constraint, or 'Thirlwall's law' (Thirlwall 1979, 2013).[7]

There is a certain growth rate, which is compatible with a balanced current account. The more exports increase with economic growth in the rest of the world, the higher is this balance-of-payments-constrained growth rate because more exports can afford a larger increase in imports. On the other hand, the more imports increase in response to a rise in income, the lower is the growth rate that balances the current account. Hence, while an equilibrated balance of payments is important to guarantee stability and growth, it is, at the same time, a constraint to growth as well.

Thirlwall's law clearly reveals the difference between key currencies and non-key currencies. Countries with international key currencies (reserve currencies) do not rely on an external source of finance to make international payments. Demand for a key currency not only depends on the originating country's exports and imports but also on all other countries' needs to settle their payments with this currency. Even if a key currency's country runs a large external deficit, the currency keeps being demanded in the foreign exchange market. Key currencies thus enjoy much more stability in terms of their exchange rate. From this it follows that reserve currency countries do not have to worry too much about current account deficits. They do not

---

[7] To be precise, Thirlwall's law says that the balance of payments constrained growth rate is given by the ratio of the income elasticity of export demand to the income elasticity of import demand multiplied by foreign income growth. See Thirlwall (1979, 2013).

need foreign currency to finance it but can provide the required finance by their own banking system.

Needless to say, this 'exorbitant privilege' (Eichengreen 2011) accrues to the United States while other currencies such as the Euro and the Chinese renminbi have a similar status at a regional level. For this reason, the balance of payments constraint is particularly relevant for developing countries because their currencies are not even a regional key currency (and by no means a global key currency). For any international payment, poor countries depend on foreign currency.

6.7 Global Markets Make Economic Policy Powerless

There are two options to relax the external constraint. On the one hand, if there are capital inflows such as foreign direct investment or even speculative capital, a country is provided with foreign currency. It can afford more imports without getting indebted and thereby without putting pressure on the exchange rate. The growth rate consistent with an equilibrated balance of payments thus is higher. However, it should be kept in mind that such capital inflows can be risky because their outflow may follow on step depending on investors' perceptions of uncertainty and profitability. Moreover, foreign direct investment may also involve subsequent capital outflows if foreign investors transfer profits to their home countries.

A second option is to increase exports via an improvement in international competitiveness. Therefore, a country has to lower its production costs entailing a depreciation of the real exchange rate as the price level declines relative to prices in the rest of the world. Higher exports then allow for higher imports and hence a higher growth rate. Yet, to the extent that competitiveness is improved via a cut in wages, economic growth is constrained again because effective demand contracts. Competitiveness gain via a mere nominal depreciation, on the other hand, means that imports become more expensive. For each imported good, the trade deficit is larger. This lowers the growth rate allowed by the external constraint again. The more effective way to relax the balance of payments constraint is competitiveness gains through productivity growth. More on this is following in a moment.

To raise the rate of economic growth, effective demand and profitability must be strong. To achieve this, different growth regimes may be envisaged (see for instance Bhaduri and Marglin 1990; Blecker 1989). Wage-led growth aims to strengthen demand via increasing wages. In this view, demand stemming from consumption expenditures out of wage income is considered as the main growth engine. Profit-led growth targets profitability and acts on the assumption that sufficient profits are the key to boost investment. We have argued in abundance that both effective demand and profitability are necessary conditions. In a given moment, one regime may be superior to the other but in the long term, they are competing strategies. The decision for either one of the regimes thus tries to exploit a trade-off between higher wages and higher profits. In the literature, this is assessed by investigating the effect of a change in the share of wages in total income. If an increase in the wage share increases economic growth, an economy is wage-led whereas it is profit-led in the opposite case. The optimal wage rate thus would maximize growth. Such considerations should, however, not give the impression that macroeconomic finetuning of the wage rate is possible. Debates on wage-led and profit-led growth rather collect arguments whether an increase of wages in an economy should be enforced or not.

Both wage-led and profit-led growth have in common that to the extent that they are successful, both of them increase net imports. Both higher wages and higher profits are tantamount to higher income, which is partially spent on goods from abroad. Hence, while both growth regimes may achieve an increase in economic growth, they are not able to do so by keeping trade balanced. The consequential current account deficit increases external indebtedness and tends to involve a currency depreciation.

A possible way out of this dilemma may be provided by another growth regime, that is, export-led growth. In the open economy, not only wage and profit income are sources of demand but also exports. While contributing to economic growth, exports help achieve a current account surplus. As has just been explained, exports are a factor to relax the external constraint. However, export-led growth is not the panacea that removes all bottlenecks in economic development. One option to get internationally competitive is by keeping wages low. While this promotes exports, it restricts demand in the domestic economy. The alternative is to reduce production costs via productivity growth. Yet, the latter requires investment, which at least in the short to middle term may give rise to a trade deficit since capital goods have to be imported. Whereas productivity growth may basically be a solution, it is exactly what many developing countries are missing today. To realize it, current account deficits may be necessary, which hits the external constraint, thus representing a macroeconomic barrier to development.

In the long term, permanent export surpluses may be attractive for one country. Yet, from a global perspective, one country's surpluses are other countries' deficits. While such a growth regime may work for one country, it involves macroeconomic instabilities at a global level. It involves that some countries pile up external debt in order to absorb other countries' external surpluses. At some point, the deficit countries cannot afford the debt service anymore. While the crisis in the Eurozone gives a particular and well-known case of the devastating effects of such imbalances, the Global South also provides more than enough examples such as those described in the introduction to this book. These instabilities may fall back to surplus countries in times of economic crises because the deficit countries eventually lack the purchasing power to exert demand for more imports.

A strong export orientation bears an additional risk. Namely, if many developing countries target the same export market in industrialized countries, the market's capacity to absorb the exports may be too small. Developing countries thus might end up with overcapacity in their export sector.

Moreover, export orientation may lead to the phenomenon called 'Dutch disease'.[8] If there is a specific good for which demand increases, those countries exporting that good enjoy higher export returns. The high goods price contributes to a current account surplus. A surplus tends to appreciate a currency through investment and capital flows to the booming economy. Furthermore, the additional money available stemming from the windfall extra export returns triggers additional demand in the domestic economy, which may give way to higher inflation and hence a further real appreciation of the exchange rate.

Such a Dutch disease effect can basically concern any sector. In many cases, and particularly in developing countries, it is triggered by internationally traded commodities. Their prices are highly volatile and in times of high global economic growth, high commodity prices are a reflection of strong demand. According to Ricardo's theory of comparative advantage, every country should focus on the sector where it is best at. For this reason, it is not surprising that non-industrialized developing countries are recommended to export agricultural and mining commodities. Yet, the Dutch disease shows the disadvantage of such commodity booms: even though it appears as a positive sign, currency appreciation and the increase in prices mean that the other sectors in the concerned country are less competitive in the global market. It becomes very hard to develop a manufacturing sector since the barrier to competitiveness is high. In the long term, the Dutch disease may hamper productivity development and thereby limit the growth potential. Exchange rate pegging could partially prevent this effect but would come with the well-known drawbacks.

Domestic demand or export orientation: whatever growth strategy is chosen, it meets its limits since the balance of payments constraint is faced as soon as economic growth increases above growth in the rest of the world. Export-led growth may overcome this restriction in the middle to long term but still is exposed to it as long as export sectors require investment expenditures. The latter usually require imports of capital goods.

The external constraint is even tighter than these arguments reveal. We have shown that markets alone are not able to initiate a development process in poor countries. Active economic policy is required. State intervention by, say, public investment meets the same limit since the economic growth it generates cannot go beyond the rate allowed by an equilibrated balance of payments. But even before economic policy gets the chance to unfold its impact, it runs the risk of being punished by capital flight. Capital flight means a loss of resources, a loss of foreign currency, and exchange rate depreciation. A process of capital flight, specifically if it is self-enforcing, violates the stability condition of an equilibrated balance of payments in the worst way. Since intervening economic policy can involve higher taxes or lower private profits when the public sector gets active in new sectors, the transfer of wealth abroad may punish it before it is even implemented.

---

[8] For more explanations on term and content, see Corden and Neary (1982).

Developing countries in global capitalism thus do not seem to have many options. Strong political commitments to successful poverty reduction induce capital flight. And even if economic policy is in line with mainstream expectations and demands of international financial markets such that capital does not see a necessity to flee out of the country, economic growth is restricted by the external constraint due to its impact on imports. Policy intervention as part of an active development strategy is rather powerless.

Box 6.2 The Devastating Effects of Capital Flight

Economic growth in countries hit by the Asian crisis in 1997 recovered soon after, although at lower levels, while governments improved financial super-vision and spurred export-led development. Yet, there are other examples showing the limits for development in a global economy more drastically especially when progressive policy is involved. The Jamaican experience with Michael Manley as prime minister from 1972 to 1980 is one of them. Manley started his term with redistribution policies by implementing a minimum wage, free education, a land reform, and other measures. The increased public spending went along with an external deficit, thus triggering currency deval-uation and inflation. The situation was exacerbated by capital flight as money aimed to evade Manley's interventionist policy.

The sharp economic contraction led to heavy violence between street gangs. Manley's government did not achieve a lasting improvement in peo-ple's living conditions during its term but was eventually faced with serious macroeconomic instability. After his electoral loss in 1980, Manley returned to office in 1989. While there were still some social reforms, the overall policy framework was a neoliberal one focusing on economic liberalization in vari-ous areas. Certainly, different sources, such as the demise of the Soviet Union, contributed to this policy change. But after the experience in the 1970s showing the limits of intervening economic policy, it is not surprising that Manley envisaged a different strategy for his second try.

Venezuela is probably the example showing the limits of intervening economic strategies best as it unfortunately expresses almost all the negative consequences that can be imagined in this regard.[9] Hugo Chavez became the country's president in 1998 and after some time he announced the 'Bolivarian Revolution' as a socialist transformation of the economy and society. The first years were marked by political turbulence and the opposition trying to over-throw the Chavez government. Such political uncertainty triggered capital flight with the central bank trying to defend the exchange rate without success. After the consolidation of power, the government faced a favorable

(continued)

---

[9]For a macroeconomic overview, see Vera (2017).

Box 6.2 (continued)

development in the form of increasing oil prices starting in 2003. This helped overcome the economic downturn.

In the following phase of growth, revenues of the public oil company were used to fund social expenditures. They featured considerable success as poverty was reduced by about 17 percentage points (Vera 2015, p. 543). Yet, capital flight continued and even increased in line with current account surpluses. Moreover, gains of foreign currency from oil exports were less and less transmitted to the central bank's reserves but used for the government spending programs. At the same time, those high levels of spending constantly pushed inflation to double-digit rates. With the nominal exchange rate pegged by the central bank, inflation means a less competitive real exchange rate. All these factors contributed to current account deficits once the oil price fell in 2008 and, again after a high-price period, in 2014. The seemingly ever-increasing oil price had covered the serious shortcomings in the external account of the Venezuelan economy. But now, the deteriorating current account and capital flight consumed currency reserves and raised foreign indebtedness. The government tried to improve the trade balance by imposing import restrictions. One of the consequences was a lack of intermediate inputs for domestic production, thus further leading to economic contraction and scarcity of goods. Moreover, there were exchange restrictions that regulated access to foreign currency from the central bank, hence a specific type of capital controls. They gave way to the creation of a shadow foreign exchange market as the need for foreign currency, namely US dollars, was tremendously high. On this shadow market, the domestic currency is traded at much weaker terms than the official exchange rate. Since 2010, successive currency devaluations have been necessary with the effect of accelerating inflation and hence further economic contraction. Poverty in Venezuela has climbed steeply again.

To avoid such experience and ensure currency stability, several developing countries, like Ecuador in 2000 and Zimbabwe in 2015, introduced the US dollar as their official currency. However, dollarization implies the complete loss of monetary scope of action.

South Africa provides another example of how capital flight can jeopardize policy. Data show that capital flight was higher between 1994 and 2000 than from 1986 to 1993 (Mohammed and Finnoff 2005). The breakpoint between these time periods was the time when the Apartheid regime was replaced by a new government under President Nelson Mandela. The data point to the conjecture that the economic elite did not trust the new post-Apartheid government and hence wanted to transfer wealth abroad to places they considered as safer.

It is extremely difficult to quantify capital flight. There are measures that, despite far from being perfect, give a helpful indication. For instance, it is

(continued)

Box 6.2 (continued)
estimated that 30 representative African countries lost 1.4 trillion US dollars from 1970 to 2015 through capital flight. If interest returns on this capital are included, the sum even amounts to 1.8 trillion (Ndikumana and Boyce 2018). Financial flows away from Africa are bigger than those flowing to the continent.

6.8 Trade and Financial Liberalization Cannot Solve the Problem

We now have a clear idea of the macroeconomic situation in which developing countries find themselves. They face a hard dilemma between active economic policy and growth on the one hand and macroeconomic stability as required by the external constraint on the other hand. Are the mainstream recipes for development that we have introduced at the beginning a useful solution? Can liberalization of trade and financial flows achieve both growth and stability?

Regarding trade, we have already shown that the conception of exchange cannot explain economic growth if the production process is ignored. At the international level, the problem replicates itself. Trade facilitates access to goods a country is not able to produce itself. It may also help with technology transfer from industrialized to developing countries even though it is rather unclear how strong this beneficial impact of trade actually is. However, and crucially, trade liberalization still does not give an answer to the question where the traded goods come from. Production is and remains the essential point. There is no reason to assume that with liberalized trade relationships, conditions for production are the best. There is no comparative cost advantage that automatically generates an equilibrated trade balance. Instead, cost advantages are absolute. Countries with lower production costs tend to have lasting trade surpluses.

In the manufacturing sector, developing countries are not able to compete with advanced economies since their productivity in manufacturing is low. Due to low wages, they are more competitive in labor-intensive sectors such as agriculture. The alternative thus is the export of natural resources such as agricultural and mining produce. This is an optimal situation according to the theory of free trade because in this way, countries do what they are best at. Yet, besides the fact that balanced trade hardly occurs, it also means that there are no market forces, which are able to change anything about this international labor division. With liberalized trade, it is likely that developing countries are stuck in exporting primary goods. Free trade does not provide them with the means to develop productivity and employ it to society's wellbeing. In the words of development economist Ha-Joon Chang (2006, pp. 33–34), the theory of comparative advantage tells us where countries are today, that is, what they are best at now. But it does not have anything to tell us about what countries may potentially achieve in the future.

We mentioned the example of textiles. If all clothes are imported, people in poor countries benefit from cheaper prices. However, no value is produced in those countries. Money leaves the country in exchange for imports while neither a productive base nor any income is created that would provide the foundation of higher living standards in the long run.

To achieve a higher productive potential, the focus has to be on production. This requires economic policy in the sense we have described it in abundance here. Trade can be a useful vehicle to strengthen productive forces in a developing country. When countries specialize in specific sectors, they can achieve economies of scale. Moreover, and needless to say, access to necessary foreign goods is an important factor to build supply chains. But trade should not be considered as of higher priority than production itself. Instead, trade policy should be employed to serve the creation of manufacturing capacity. In some instances, protection of infant industries with tariffs is required. This is often the only way to steer productivity because industrial sectors need time to build knowhow, apply technologies and create organizational as well as administrative efficiency. On the other hand, too much protection may be harmful if it removes any pressure on an industry to become more productive over time. Moreover, too much protectionism may also deny access to export markets in other countries as they employ tariffs and other trade restrictions as well.

If goods markets in developing countries are totally exposed to global markets via trade liberalization, trade deficits can be even larger than in the case of some protection since the propensity of income to import is likely to be higher with liberalized trade. This is partially due to foreign goods becoming cheaper for consumers. Moreover, since trade liberalization may jeopardize infant industries in developing countries, those goods have to be imported. For any increase of domestic incomes, deindustrialization thus makes imports increase more strongly than in the absence of trade liberalization. The risk of foreign indebtedness and exchange rate depreciation may thus increase. Hence, instead of steering economic growth, trade liberalization can even contribute to a lower balance-of-payments-constrained growth rate. This has actually been confirmed by empirical research (Pacheco-López and Thirlwall 2007).

Financial liberalization, that is, the reduction of barriers to capital flows, does not alter the external constraint in a sustainable way either. With a liberalized capital account, financial inflows in times of economic booms allow a country to make investments and finance imports. However, as mentioned several times the sudden reversal of capital flows involves exchange rate volatility that, if strong enough, the central bank of a country can hardly counter. Even though mainstream theory claims that financial liberalization allows capital to be internationally allocated in the most efficient way, it is by no means clear that capital flows serve the needs of a country best.

Compared to short-run oriented speculative financial flows, foreign direct investment has a more stable and longer-term perspective. A foreign loan may possibly serve the purpose of providing long-run finance just as well. Capital flows are driven by interest rate differentials, profit expectations, speculation. Uncertainty, and the instability resulting from it, plays an essential role. The liberalization of capital flows thus is a source of additional instability because it gives more space to uncertainty and profit expectations that are guided away from productive investments. This is why it is far from clear that financial liberalization increases foreign direct investment. Rather than real investment, capital flows might find a source of short-term profits in speculative activities in the foreign exchange market more easily. This might actually harm foreign direct investment.

But even apart from the risk of short-term speculative flows, financial liberalization may also be harmful in the long term. Having assessed that profitability is an essential driver of economic growth, we can also make a conclusion by going in the opposite direction. High growth rates may have specific causes across countries. But we can confidentially say that in these countries (at least as what concerns their private sectors) the profitability condition, and also the demand condition, is fulfilled. Otherwise, growth performance would be less good. Developing countries stagnate because they do not have sufficient profitable investment opportunities for investors. This is why capital flows go in those countries with higher rates of profits, interest and growth—completely in line with the determinants of exchange rate changes we have identified at the beginning of this chapter.

Financial liberalization thus may induce not just short-term flows but also increase the long-run tendency of capital flowing out of developing countries to advanced economies. This is what is observed in real-world data (see Box 6.2). In a nutshell, even though liberalization opens the door for capital inflows, the foreign guests may prefer not to enter. On the other hand, the open door also allows domestic capital to leave the house.

Mainstream prescriptions for developing countries are no solution to the macroeconomic dilemma between growth and stability. Additionally, we have to admit that capital inflows to finance economic growth and exchange rate pegging are not a perfect response either. Finally, capital controls are a way to direct those flows such that they are employed in productive rather than speculative use. Yet, capital controls are imperfect. While they may be a barrier to a sudden tightening of the external constraint by preventing or slowing down capital flight, they cannot relax it in the long term.

References

Bhaduri A, Marglin S (1990) Unemployment and the real wage: the economic basis for contesting political ideologies. Cambridge J Econ 14:375–393. https://doi.org/10.1093/oxfordjournals.cje.a035141

Blecker RA (1989) International competition, income distribution and economic growth. Cambridge J Econ 13(3):395–412. https://doi.org/10.1093/oxfordjournals.cje.a035100

Blecker RA, Setterfield M (2019) Heterodox macroeconomics: models of demand, distribution and growth. Edward Elgar, Cheltenham and Northampton

Cencini A (2000) World monetary disorders: exchange rate erratic fluctuations. Centro di Studi Bancari Quaderni di Ricerca, No. 2. http://doc.rero.ch/record/28437?ln=it

Cencini A, Schmitt B (1991) External debt servicing: a vicious circle. Pinter Publishers, London

Chang H-J (2006) The east Asian development experience: the miracle, the crisis and the future. Penang, Zed Books Ltd. and Third World Network, London

Corden WM, Neary JP (1982) Booming sector and de-industrialisation in a small open economy. Econ J 92(368):825–848. https://doi.org/10.2307/2232670

Dornbusch R (1976) Expectations and exchange rate dynamics. J Polit Econ 84(6):1161–1176

Eichengreen B (2011) Exorbitant privilege: the rise and fall of the dollar. Oxford University Press, Oxford

Marx K (1894/2004) Das Kapital. Kritik der politischen Ökonomie, dritter Band. Akademie Verlag, Berlin

Mishkin FS (1998) The dangers of exchange-rate pegging in emerging-market countries. Int Finance 1(1):81–101. https://doi.org/10.1111/1468-2362.00005

Mohammed S, Finnoff K (2005) Capital flight from South Africa, 1980–2000. In: Epstein G (ed) Capital flight and capital controls in developing countries. Edward Elgar, Cheltenham, pp 85–115

Mohanty M (2014) International transmission of monetary policy – an overview. Bank for International Settlement Papers, No 78, 1–24. https://www.bis.org/publ/bppdf/bispap78.htm

Ndikumana L, Boyce JK (2018) Capital flight from Africa: updated methodology and new estimates. Political Economy Research Institute, University of Massachusetts Amherst, Research Report. https://peri.umass.edu/publication/item/1083-capital-flight-from-africa-updated-methodology-and-new-estimates

Pacheco-López P, Thirlwall AP (2007) Trade liberalisation and the trade-off between growth and the balance of payments in Latin America. Int Rev Appl Econ 21(4):469–490. https://doi.org/10.1080/02692170701474587

Rogoff K (2002) Rethinking capital controls: when should we keep an open mind? Finance Dev 39(4):55–56. https://international.vlex.com/vid/rethinking-controls-keep-open-mind-41415890

Rueff J (1963) Gold exchange standard: a danger to the west. In: Grubel HD (ed) World monetary reform. Plans and issues. Stanford University Press and Oxford University Press, Stanford and London, pp 320–328

Shaikh A (2016) Capitalism: competition, conflict, crises. Oxford University Press, New York

Thirlwall AP (1979) The balance of payments constraint as an explanation of international growth rates differences. Banca Nazionale Lavoro Q Rev 32(128):45–53

Thirlwall AP (2013) Economic growth in an open developing economy: the role of structure and demand. Edward Elgar, Cheltenham

Vera L (2015) Venezuela 1999–2014: macro-policy, oil governance and economic performance. Comp Econ Stud 57:539–568. https://doi.org/10.1057/ces.2015.13

Vera L (2017) In search of stabilization and recovery: macro policy and reforms in Venezuela. J post Keynesian Econ 40(1):9–26. https://doi.org/10.1080/01603477.2016.1273069

Chapter 7
Reclaiming Economic Policy

Global Markets constrain economic policy in an individual country. Given this conclusion, taking recourse to Washington Consensus-like recommendations may be the best way out. We have shown that the market left alone hardly ever brings about long-term development in poor countries. Yet, compared to state-led development one may argue that the neoliberal policy prescriptions of trade and financial liberalization trigger fewer negative consequences.

It is definitely easy to take a fatalist stance favoring unregulated markets by claiming that it is the only useful alternative. However, there are other options, which do not merely allow for more optimism but also have a better analytical foundation than neoclassical macroeconomics.

According to our previous analysis, we know that a solution to the macroeconomic problems of developing countries must include a mechanism that does not make countries' development depend on external balance or surpluses. In Chap. 5, it has been shown how policy intervention in the form of appropriate spending plans and public investment is able to drive economic growth. Active economic policy and the government as a macroeconomic agent are the key to escape poor countries' state of stagnation due to a lack of effective demand and profitability. However, the balance of payments constraint and, in particular, capital flight set tight limits to the realization of progressive policy programs. A successful macroeconomic strategy for a country thus must be able to give back the required space to economic policy irrespective of what happens to the country's current account.

Let us, first, have a look at the international payment system once again. The proper analysis of international payments is key to the understanding of the external constraint and the creation of a better solution.

B. Oberholzer, *Fighting Global Poverty*, SpringerBriefs in Economics,
https://doi.org/10.1007/978-3-658-36631-5_7

7.1   Interest on External Debt Is Paid Twice

Popular understanding of international payments is as follows. We take the example of a firm, which imports goods such as, say, medicaments. To make the payment to the foreign seller, the firm has to access foreign reserves since the bill of the imports is due in foreign currency. It offers domestic currency that it has either earned from past sales or received by getting indebted to the bank where it has a deposit. The bank provides the firm with the foreign currency by taking it from either its own reserves or by borrowing it from the central bank reserves. Hence, the importing firm and the bank exchange domestic and foreign currency. The firm thus can use the foreign currency to make the payment. This process takes place whenever an importer gives a payment order to a bank.

As reasonable as it looks at a first glance, this perception is wrong. Let us refer to the explanation of exchange rate fluctuations in the previous chapter again. There, it has been shown what happens when a country with its own domestic currency receives a payment from abroad. The bank, or the banking system, respectively, receives the payment in foreign currency while the domestic payee is endowed with a deposit of newly created money in domestic currency. The bank's balance sheet grows. This describes the case of exports or other financial inflows. Let us now come back to the case of imports where a payment to the rest of the world has to be made.

This step is crucial to be understood. When the importing firm pays for imports, it does so by spending its own deposit in domestic currency. At the same time, the payment is due in foreign currency. The bank (the banking system) thus exerts this payment by either using its reserves or by accessing an external loan. Let us assume the latter case for now. While the importer pays in domestic currency, the bank makes the payment in foreign money. However, the bank does not receive the payment of the importing firm. What happens is the following thing: first, when the payment for imports takes place, the money denominated in foreign currency disappears from the bank's balance sheet. This is the payment to the foreign exporter, hence straightforward. Second, the money in domestic currency paid by the importer is the counterpart of the payment in international currency. Therefore, like the foreign currency the deposit in domestic currency disappears from the bank's balance sheet. Where does it go? The answer is: nowhere. Just like deposits in domestic currency are created out of nothing when a resident of the country receives a payment from abroad, deposits are destroyed when payments to the rest of the world have to be made. This money is lost to the economy.

This finding contradicts conventional wisdom, but it is what actually happens in today's system of international payments. The French economist Bernard Schmitt has elaborated the far-reaching consequences arising from the results of this analysis.[1] Indeed, we cannot just take this observation as a natural issue not to worry about. The problem of today's payment structure is that payments for imports are made twice. The payment in domestic currency and the one in foreign currency are

---

[1] For the most extensive analysis, see Schmitt (2014).

not the same but, as a matter of fact, add to one another. There are different ways to prove this. We limit ourselves to an explanation as simple as possible.

It is easy to understand that reference to a foreign loan to pay for imports represents an increase in external debt. But what about the money paid by the importing firm itself in domestic currency? In the national economy, money comes into existence when a bank grants a loan to a firm such that the latter can pay workers and start producing goods. Money thus is tied to economic production. Creation of output and creation of money go hand in hand so that the latter measures the former in terms of monetary units. So far, so good; the principles of endogenous money and the monetary circuit have been explained above.

Now, when money is spent for imports instead of goods in the domestic economy, a corresponding share of those domestic goods remains unsold. The same corresponding part of debt that was created to produce those goods cannot be repaid because the required sales returns are missing. Due to the payment made for the imports, the money needed to generate those sales returns is lost to the economy. This means that effective demand in the domestic economy shrinks such that, eventually, output falls. In fact, it falls by the amount of the imports. In this sense, the payment for imports doubles since there is a monetary as well as a real payment. The payments in domestic and foreign currencies are not the same but add to one another. Hence, the importing country pays once by running into a foreign debt. This debt has to be repaid by exporting the respective amount of goods sometime in the future, which will provide the currency revenues required. The importing country pays a second time, via the loss of monetary units in its own currency, by cutting its own domestic demand, and thus its output. In other words again, the country sacrifices once a part of its future output (to be exported) and once a part of its current output.

To the extent that imports are compensated by exports in the same period, no double payment takes place because exports and imports involve opposite payments. While imports require a double payment, exports give rise to a duplication of money since the exporting country receives both foreign reserves and creates new money in domestic currency. These two duplications cancel each other out when exports and imports are balanced. The twofold payment thus applies to the extent that a country runs a trade deficit or, by adding the trade unrelated payments, a current account deficit.

External debt involves interest in foreign currency. This allows us to discover the double charge of external debt from a different perspective. As we have argued, external debt servicing triggers an exchange rate devaluation when foreign currency has to be purchased in the foreign exchange market. Hence, paying the interest in foreign currency involves a first payment. Demand for foreign currency in the foreign exchange market rises relative to supply corresponding to the amount of the interest. To undo the currency devaluation, the central bank would have to intervene by releasing an amount of reserves equal to the interest payment such that the original relation between supply and demand in the foreign exchange market is reestablished. This is the second payment.

These two explanations of the duplication of external debt and debt servicing are different in the sense that the second one with interest payments involves exchange rate fluctuations and transactions in the foreign exchange market while the first one does not. However, both explanations involve a few steps in a bookkeeping balance sheet to end up at the same result. Without going further into details here, we see that the problem of the double payment arising from external deficits has many dimensions that are interlinked.

7.2   Deficit Countries in a Vicious Cycle

The mechanism of the double payment of current account deficits, though not easy to understand, has serious consequences. It leads to growing external debt on which interest is due. Deficit countries thus have to make surplus exports in the future to service debt and to repay foreign loans. This is not extraordinary. However, due to the current payment structure, current account deficits involve an exchange rate devaluation. Moreover, the double payment of net imports means that deficit countries lose resources since domestic demand and employment shrink. The more external debt accumulates, the harder it becomes for a country to keep up economic activity. However, the latter is the source out of which the exports must be generated in order to earn foreign currency for debt service and repayment. In a world of appropriate macroeconomic governance, the opposite should apply. Countries with a current account deficit should gain resources, maybe even at a faster pace than surplus countries, instead of losing them. This would allow those deficit countries to establish and improve the economy's productive foundation such that they can become stronger in export markets and rebalance their current account soon.

The current international monetary structure has emerged after the abandon of the Bretton Woods system of fixed exchange rates at the beginning of the 1970s. The Bretton Woods regime had been established after World War II.[2] Apart from the foundation of the World Bank and the International Monetary Fund, its main feature was the pegging of exchange rates to the US dollar whereas the US dollar was backed by gold intending to secure its value. This went well as long as the United States ran current account surpluses, which they were willing to reinvest in the deficit countries. It allowed for the final settlement of trade flows thanks to which the deficit countries had no major trouble financing their net imports. In this way, exchange rate stability could be maintained.

However, the US current account exhibited growing external deficits in the 1960s meaning that the surplus countries started piling up US dollar reserves. This implied that it became increasingly difficult for the United States to credibly guarantee the US dollar's value by its gold reserves. After the escalation of the conflict the

[2]For a more extensive historical background of the Bretton Woods System, see Varoufakis et al. (2011).

exchange rate peg was eventually abandoned with currencies floating freely from then on.

Among heterodox economists, the post Bretton Woods system is often referred to as an actual 'non-system' of international payments since there is no global architecture that would regulate the floating of exchange rates. The term is appropriate. However, the mechanism of double payment for external debt servicing usually going unnoticed in the economic debate reveals that the consequences of the non-system are far worse than the conventional debate suggests. Furthermore, even the Bretton Woods system faced the same shortcoming since as we know by now, exchange rate pegging does not change anything about the bookkeeping mechanics of international payments.

Let us compare payments between countries to those within a country to once again see the harmful effects of the current international monetary structure's flaws. For this, we have to distinguish between two conceptions of the economy. On the one hand, an economy is the sum of its residents. These residents are households, firms, the state, banks, and whoever plays a role in economic activity. On the other hand, the economy is defined by its currency space. In this regard, it comprises all economic activities taking place by using the currency issued by the economy's national banking system. While the former definition refers to the sum of microeconomic agents, the latter is truly macroeconomic since it does not rely on individuals. The first definition focuses on the structure composed of the individual agents and the relationships between them whereas the second looks at the economy from the angle of the monetary circuit of the currency space irrespective of the characteristics of agents involved in it.

Both conceptions are correct. Nevertheless, their distinction is important for a specific reason. When, say, a firm pays wages to workers within the same economy, the procedure is simple. The money is transferred from the firm's account to the workers' accounts. Independent of whether the payments take place within the same bank or between different banks, the size of the total banking system's balance sheet does not change. While there is a transfer between residents, that is, a microeconomic payment, the overall currency space is not affected.

Things change when payments become international. Let us assume that firms pay for imported production inputs. It is again a microeconomic payment since money flows from one microeconomic agent to another one. However, since the payee is not a resident of the country, the currency space is also affected. The mechanism involved in such an international payment regarding the destruction of domestic currency and the need to pay with foreign currency now enters the scene. Hence, the microeconomic payment entails a second, a macroeconomic, payment, which means that the sum of domestic currency available decreases while external debt increases.

The difference between national and international payments can be described in less technical terms: while a payment within the economy only concerns the payer and the payee, international payments additionally involve the macroeconomic system as a whole. The effects of external deficits like currency depreciation, inflation, loss of economic resources, and increase in external debt harm everyone in the economy concerned. Therefore, not only the payer and the payee are concerned, but all residents of an economy suffer from payments made between merely two agents. The fact that every international payment has macroeconomic consequences is a harmful mistake in the current international monetary 'non-system'.

From the previous chapter, we know that developing countries do not have the chance to import investment goods to the extent that they cause a current account deficit. They could afford it by relying on capital inflows for a while and to some extent. But apart from this, external deficits give way to the instability regarding exchange rate, inflation and foreign debt. The external constraint has even worse consequences than described in the previous chapter since the double payment of external deficits also deprives countries of the resources they need to run surpluses in the future.

Yet, the story does not have to end here. As bad as the situation seems, it is precisely the analysis of the duplication of international payments, which provides the foundation for a solution to the external debt problem.

Box 7.1 Developing Countries and the Covid-19 Pandemic

The Covid-19 pandemic, originating in China at the end of 2019 and after having spread all over the world about 4 months later, provides object teaching of the devastating effects of international financial turbulences on developing countries. Once it became clear that the coronavirus would not only affect tourism and mobility but also household spending in advanced countries, stock prices crashed. Demand for energy plummeted since air transport was cut down due to strict travelling restrictions at country borders. At the same time, lockdowns within countries left local traffic and transport at a fraction of their usual level. International trade was heavily affected as not only passenger transport but also goods traffic was constrained. Investment plans were postponed. As a consequence, the oil price fell to a record low, going even into negative territory for a short time in April 2020. Similar drastic price drops occurred in the markets for commodities such as copper, aluminum, soybeans, coffee, cocoa, cotton, and most other primary material.

On the one hand, this was caused by maximum uncertainty with respect to demand for those commodities during the lockdown but also regarding the unknown duration of this unprecedented shock and the heavy clouds on long-term economic development. On the other hand, these commodities are highly financialized meaning that they are subject to a high volume of transactions by financial investors. The steep fall in prices of financial assets also meant that investors withdrew from commodity futures markets. Lower commodity prices thus at least partially also reflected the implosion of speculative activity.

Low commodity prices imply falling export returns for developing countries whose exports are usually mostly made up of primary commodities.

(continued)

Box 7.1 (continued)

Hence, in this particular situation where advanced economies were forced to slow down and struggled to keep up industrial production, the shock wave multiplied as it arrived in developing countries. Additionally, poor countries had to impose their own lockdowns, thus jeopardizing fragile industries and other sectors. Prospects of lower export returns pointed to future balance of payments problems. The consequence of this would be tight supply of foreign currency and, hence, a currency devaluation.

Moreover, shrunk opportunities in the domestic economies led to a reversal of foreign investment flows. Both these expectations and actual effects triggered immediate outflows of capital from developing countries and made exchange rate depreciation a reality. In emerging economies, where more data is available, capital flight reached about 100 billion US dollars within a month in spring 2020, a multiple of the flows after the financial crisis in 2008; some currencies devalued by as much as 20% (OECD 2020).

Advanced economies supported their economies by unseen monetary policy measures. The central banks of the US, the European Union and China started quantitative easing programs beyond the purchase of government bonds by now including private bonds as well as direct loans to non-financial companies. These measures created spillovers as the abundance of financial capital gave way to new flows to emerging and possibly also developing countries, which counteracted capital flight partially. Moreover, the Federal Reserve of the US extended its swap lines and established new ones with central banks from emerging economies. This means that it provided US dollars in exchange against currency of the respective countries. In a similar way, it established so-called repo facilities where countries could access US dollars by providing US Treasury bonds. In total, these measures increased dollar availability in foreign exchange markets. This made the defense of exchange rates for emerging economies easier. While developing countries did not get direct access to US dollar swap lines, it is likely that they were able to benefit from a spillover of dollar availability in the foreign exchange market.

Ultra-expansive monetary policies in advanced economies may have eased pressure on developing countries' balance of payments a bit. However, it did not change anything about the fundamental problem, which means that capital flight implies increasing external indebtedness. Foreign debt had been on the rise for many developing countries even before the pandemic and may now definitely end up in a new debt crisis. G20 countries decided on a relief on debt service for 2020, which, however, changes nothing about the stock of debt. Zambia was the first country to announce a partial default on its foreign debt in November 2020. Many more countries are currently negotiating with the IMF and other international creditors.

(continued)

Box 7.1 (continued)

At the time of writing of these paragraphs, the global macroeconomic situation remains as uncertain as hardly ever before. The future course of the pandemic, the evolution of the coronavirus and the success of vaccination campaigns are unknown. Commodity prices have reincreased partially or completely. Yet, it is hard to tell whether this informs about the future economic recovery. It is likely that the new peaks in financial markets caused by quantitative easing also pushed up commodity prices. This questions the sustainability of the rebound of developing countries' export prices.

7.3   The Keynes Plan

At Bretton Woods conference in 1944, the debate was about how to structure the international payment system in order to prevent systemic crises arising from trade imbalances. Keynes, as the leading negotiator on behalf of the United Kingdom, proposed a design now known as the Keynes plan. At the center of this proposal, there is a kind of international central bank, called the International Clearing Union. It issues an international currency, the bancor, that countries use to settle foreign payments. Whenever a country runs a current account deficit, it is endowed with the bancor units required to make the payments while the country's international account at the clearing union is debited with the corresponding amount. On the other hand, a surplus country earns international currency credited on its international account. This reform brings about some important progress. Compared to today's (non-)system of international payments where countries have to access US dollars to pay for imports, in Keynes's plan international currency is not scarce for deficit countries since it is provided by the clearing union at a defined exchange rate and at whatever amount needed.

So far, Keynes's design does not rule out balance of payments disequilibria. To take this problem into account, the plan includes a fine that is imposed on imbalances and increases with the size of the imbalance. However, if deficit countries were penalized for their 'overconsumption', they would have to reduce imports by cutting down expenditures in their economies. Demand would shrink from which the global economy would suffer. Therefore, the fine is imposed on surplus countries. Trade and financial imbalances involve both deficit and surplus countries. Hence, it is not appropriate to just blame the deficit countries. The balancing mechanism of the financial penalty thus is imposed where macroeconomic costs are suggested to be minimized. Beyond this, the effect of the financial fine may even be expansionary because surplus countries get an incentive to import more, which creates new export markets for the deficit countries.

But the Keynes plan also has an essential weakness: it may stabilize international trade and financial flows but it does not account for those flows' impacts on national economies. Indeed, a surplus country is credited with bancor on its international account. But as in today's monetary structure, the exporter of the respective country receives the sales return in domestic currency. Hence, the national banking system endows the exporter with newly created money in domestic currency. The overall balance sheet of the banking system grows. On the other hand, importers still pay with domestic currency while the payment to the exporting country must be made in international currency.

Even though the supply of bancor accommodates any demand for it, thus removing pressure for deficit countries, the system cannot avoid the double payment of imports. This means that the money in domestic currency paid for imports is still lost to the economy. In a nutshell, while the Keynes plan includes a steering mechanism that counteracts international trade imbalances, it neglects the mechanism involved in the bookkeeping of international payments, which itself causes and exacerbates those imbalances. Namely, the loss of domestic currency and resources that would be required to strengthen export capacity in deficit countries is not addressed.

The shortcoming of the Keynes plan can be removed by adding an essential element. It relies on a simple basic idea: if all imports are matched by real exports of an equal amount, the monetary imbalances occurring today in deficit and surplus countries will be gone. The central question thus is about how we can bring the balance of payments into equilibrium meaning a current account of zero. One may argue that external imbalances are precisely the core of the problem such that assuming them away does not help solve the problem. However, there is a way to get from imbalance to balance.

Again, a trade deficit means that a country imports more goods than it exports. This imbalance can be equilibrated by referring to the other components of the current account. Simply put, deficit in the trade of real assets can be offset by a surplus in the trade of financial assets. Those assets can basically be stocks, bonds, and other securities. In a broader and more abstract sense, these financial assets are a kind of real assets. Apart from speculative price fluctuations, the basic value of financial assets is defined by the real assets that back it and which the owners of financial assets eventually have a claim for. In this broader view, securities are a part of domestic output. When deficit countries transfer those securities abroad, it eventually means that a part of domestic output is sold. The export of these securities compensates for the surplus imports we identified as the original problem.

The completion of the Keynes plan can thus be presented as follows[3]: a deficit country receives bancor from the international clearing union and is indebted in bancor to the latter. This implies a double payment. Now, the country sells securities to the international settlement institution equal to the amount of the current account deficit. It thus earns the same number of international money units it has paid for its net imports. The balance of payments is equilibrated.

On the other side of the trade, a surplus country receives international currency, the amount of which is transferred to the account of the exporters by creation of new

---

[3]For an elaboration on Keynes's global reform and its completion, see Rossi (2015).

domestic money. To avoid this surplus money, the country eliminates its surplus by purchasing securities from the international clearing union. This involves a double payment for the surplus country since, again, the purchasers of the securities pay in domestic currency while the country's banking system settles the bill in bancor. Yet, this is not a mistake in this case since the double payment exactly compensates for the monetary duplication arising from the original external surplus. Overall, surplus countries purchase the securities sold by the deficit countries while the transfers and payments are organized by the international institution. Trade is balanced and no monetary distortions occur.

7.4   The One-Country Solution

A global solution to manage international payments may be wishful and optimal. Yet, developing countries are not able to enforce such an agreement at the international level. Furthermore, poor countries need a solution to the external constraint today rather than at an indeterminate time in the future once long-term negotiations might (or might not) have come to an end.[4] Let us therefore refer to a proposal elements of which can be found with the economist Ernst Friedrich Schumacher in his analysis of the 1940s (Schumacher 1943) and which has been developed further by Bernard Schmitt.[5] The proposal can be applied unilaterally by an individual country without depending on an international currency such as the bancor. While we have described the Keynes plan only briefly, we now have a more detailed look at the one-country reform. We summarize its structure and emphasize the elements necessary for the purpose at hand.

The one-country reform of international payments affects neither exporters nor importers, be they firms, governments or private households. Indeed, nothing changes for them so that the reform may even go unnoticed if not declared as such. Yet, its advantages are fundamental.

With the one-country solution, an institution, which settles international payments, is still needed. Following Schmitt (2014), we call it the 'bureau'. It is a public institution and can be unilaterally set up by the country that implements the reform. Whenever a resident of the country pays for imports, it does so in domestic currency. So far, nothing changes. Yet, instead of destroying these monetary units while making a second payment in foreign currency, the bank of the importer pays the

---

[4]This was already tried at the Bretton Woods conference after World War II. While the system of fixed exchange rates was established, an international clearing union as intended by the Keynes plan never came into existence. The United States preferred to decide autonomously on the reinvestment of their then external surpluses abroad instead of handing decision power of financial flows to an international organization.

[5]The following explanations of the reform are broadly based on Schmitt (2014) and Brunette (2015).

owed amount of money to the bureau. The bureau completes the payment by paying the exporter of the foreign country in foreign currency.

On the asset side of the bureau's balance sheet, we now find a deposit in domestic currency, which it received from the importer. The payment by the importer literally means that the ownership of its deposit is transferred to the bureau. Hence, for the domestic banking system, nothing changes except that the deposit is no more owned by the importer but by the bureau. The newly gained money in form of a deposit on the bureau's balance sheet is matched by debt of the same amount on its liability side. This debt arises from the payment in foreign currency for which the bureau needs to access a foreign loan.[6]

By now, the situation for the developing country is as it should be. Since the ownership of the money just changes from the importer to the bureau but is not destroyed in the course of the payment, the economy loses no money. Domestic demand and employment can be maintained as will be explained in a moment. However, there still is foreign debt, which involves the problem of how the external surplus can be achieved to pay interest and repay the debt.

This is why the bureau makes a second step, which is crucial to complete the reform. Let us express this in an abstract way first: the bureau lends back the amount it has borrowed on the financial markets in the rest of the world. At the same time, the rest of the world obtains real resources of the same amount from the deficit country. These are most likely financial securities as introduced in the draft of the global reform. Hence, like with the global reform, imports and exports are brought to the same level. From this moment, there is no more net external debt because external borrowing and lending compensate each other. In a less abstract way, the bureau emits and sells financial securities abroad, which allows it to earn the foreign currency to repay the foreign loan. Putting the words even more simply, the bureau transfers securities abroad to prevent external debt from building up. The reform is completed. Even though the current account deficit looks like an external imbalance, the reform makes it a balance.[7]

As this analysis shows, a current account deficit provides the bureau with money in domestic currency. These monetary units are essential because their existence on the bureau's balance sheet instead of their destruction ensures that effective demand and output do not shrink. However, in order to eventually have this effect, this money must not stay on the bureau's balance sheet. The bureau must spend it. Spending in the domestic economy can be either for consumption or, what is a much better way, for productive investment. Hence, the asset side of the balance sheet is modified as real assets such as capital goods replace the bank deposit. The bureau thus is not only a settlement agency for international payments, it also

---

[6]If the bureau owns foreign reserves from past current account surpluses, those could also be used for the payment. In accounting logic, this is tantamount to an increase in external debt.

[7]When referring to current account deficits and surpluses in the remainder, we mean those that would occur in the absence of the reform.

becomes an agent involved in the domestic economy. It ensures effective demand and domestic macroeconomic stability.

Important to be mentioned, the money in domestic currency received by the bureau is an extra profit. By spending it, the bureau does not incur any additional debt. It is true that the bureau's assets are matched by the securities it has transferred abroad meaning that the assets eventually are owned by foreign residents. But from a macroeconomic perspective comprising the currency space of an economy, the bureau's increase in assets from its investment are an additional income that would not have come into existence in the hitherto existing international payments (non-)system.

Example

Let us explain the mechanism of the one-country reform step by step with the example of a deficit country:

1. The importer pays in domestic currency. The bureau receives the payment.
2. Simultaneously, the bureau makes the payment to the foreign exporter in foreign currency by accessing a loan.
3. After these two steps, the bureau's balance sheet looks as follows: on its asset side, it owns a bank deposit in domestic currency. On the liability side, the bureau faces an external debt of an equal amount.
4. The bureau gives up real resources of the country, that is, it transfers financial securities to the rest of the world, which provides it with the foreign currency to repay the foreign loan.
5. The bureau's balance sheet now reveals no net external debt because the sale of securities abroad has canceled it. The bureau repays or avoids external debt by transferring resources equal to the net imports.
6. The bureau spends the extra profit in the domestic economy. By making productive investment, it creates production capacity and becomes the owner of capital goods. This means that the bureau exchanges its bank deposit in domestic currency against real assets (investment goods).
7. Finally, the bureau owns capital goods (asset side) while it faces financial securities on its liability side. However, there is no debt in foreign currency even though the securities are owned by foreign residents. Thus, the new production capacity is the gain of the country.

This description is kept as simple as possible to explain the bookkeeping process. In reality, the securities transferred abroad to rebalance the current account are not necessarily the bureau's own liabilities though this would be the simplest way. However, depending on what investment the bureau makes with the extra profits, the securities it emits may be more or less marketable as they belong to more or less liquid markets. Moreover, for political considerations such as economic sovereignty, a country may not want the bureau's capital goods to be owned by foreign investors as they may be of strategic importance to the country's development. In this case, the transfer of securities could also be administered by the central bank. It purchases securities in the domestic financial market and sells them abroad or issues central bank bonds while the bureau and the central bank settle the remaining claims bilaterally. As further varieties, the bureau may itself actually make investment decisions or it may transfer the extra profits arising from current account deficits to the government, which integrates it into its investment plan.

The following Fig. 7.1 summarizes, again in the most formal way, the monetary and financial flows occurring when a country runs a current account deficit. With the example of imports, we see that for every flow of money—be it in domestic or foreign currency—a corresponding opposite flow guarantees that monetary balance can be maintained. The domestic economy does not lose any money such that demand does not decrease. Loans of the same amount in opposite directions (once of the deficit country for surplus imports and once of the rest of the world for obtaining securities) cancel each other out. Monetary balance is ensured while payments are completed in real terms: net imports of real goods against net export of financial securities.

With the reform, all international payments are made via the bureau. Hence, domestic banks only have loans and deposits in domestic currency on their balance sheets. In a strict sense, the only 'trading partner' of domestic importers and exporters is the bureau. They pay to the bureau or get paid by it while the bureau takes charge of the final settlement of the international payment with the actual trading partner abroad. Likewise, the bureau is the only institution to pay or be paid by foreign exporters and importers, respectively. In fact, this means that the banking systems of the importing country and the exporting country settle their claims via the bureau. Nothing changes for the individual payer or payee who give payment orders and receive the payment in the bank account, respectively.

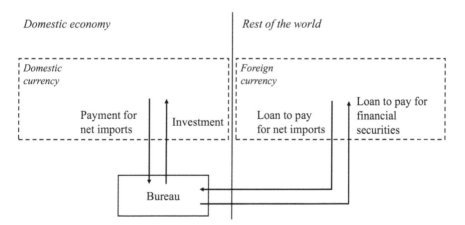

Fig. 7.1 The mechanism of the one-country reform for a deficit country

7.5   Exchange Rate Stability and A Growing Resource Pool

How does this reform bring about a fundamental change? First of all, it avoids the double payment of current account deficits and, eventually, of interest on external debt by preventing that external debt even builds up. Since the money in domestic currency used to pay for the imports is not destroyed but transferred to the bureau, the latter can reinvest it in the domestic economy as has been shown above. In today's system, the loss of domestic money means that it cannot be spent on domestic goods so that the latter go unsold. Effective demand, and thus output, decreases. Reinvestment by the bureau not only maintains demand but even contributes to production capacity, technological progress by the installation of new production plants, and hence productivity growth. The economy's resources increase instead of shrinking. This is important as it enlarges the base of real resources needed to provide to the rest of the world in times of deficits. The bigger the resource pool, the easier it is to transfer securities abroad as the latter represent a part of those resources.

Second, the reform ensures exchange rate stability. Since the bureau is now responsible for all international transactions, the domestic currency and the foreign currency are strictly separated. As a simple consequence, the foreign exchange market is abolished. Speculators cannot affect the exchange rate via purchasing and selling currencies anymore. Hence, there is no more option to try to benefit from infinitesimal exchange rate changes, which may exacerbate to self-enforcing capital flows and continuous currency depreciation or appreciation. The bureau thus can determine the exchange rate at which it settles payments between domestic and foreign residents.

This second result of the reform has an important consequence: in contrast to today's (non-)system of international payments, current account deficits do not cause exchange rate depreciations anymore. The problems of higher burden of external debt, imported inflation, and macroeconomic instability due to exchange rate fluctuations are gone. Since the exchange rate is not determined by the market anymore, it follows that it is back under the control of the government in a broader sense. It now requires a policy decision to define the relative value of the currency. This task could be the assigned responsibility of the bureau or, more likely, of the central bank. The latter does not have to defend an exchange rate target via intervention in the foreign exchange market anymore. But like with today's exchange rate pegging, the appropriate level of the exchange rate has to be identified. Depending on the development of a country's production costs relative to those of trading partners and depending on the targeted growth regime, it may be appropriate to make long-term adjustments in the exchange rate from time to time.

As a little, probably redundant, reminder, today developing countries are forced to run balanced current accounts or even surpluses at least in the middle term because otherwise currency devaluation and external indebtedness get out of control. Thanks to the reform, current account deficits and exchange rate stability are not in contradiction to each other anymore. This implies nothing less than that the balance of payments constraint is removed or at least strongly relaxed. A country, which reforms its international payments in the way described here, is allowed to run deficits without being punished by a currency crisis. For this reason, developing countries can grow faster with macroeconomic stability being ensured. The higher imports triggered by rising incomes of households do not entail an increase in external indebtedness anymore and thus do not affect the exchange rate. This happens because a current account deficit is actually not a deficit anymore even though we keep calling it like this for convenience. Any external deficit is balanced via a transfer of securities of an equal amount.

With the reform, poor countries can apply effective development strategies again. They can use monetary policy and, particularly, active economic policies such as public investment, appropriate taxes and social transfers. We have analyzed their potential from a macroeconomic perspective in Chap. 5. There, it has been shown how they can steer economic development, which markets alone cannot deliver. Unfortunately, we have also seen that policy intervention of this kind becomes largely ineffective once the economy is considered with regard to its international integration. Now, with the one-country reform of international payments, countries get their scope of action back.

So far, we have focused on the case where a country runs a current account deficit. How does the reform of international payments work when there is a surplus? Let us look at this case to complete the explanation. Nothing changes with respect to the bureau's role. It is still the only institution, which settles the payments. Let us explain this with the payment for a country's net exports. As in the current system, the importer in the foreign country pays in foreign currency. The payment is made to the bureau, which now has foreign reserves on the asset side of its balance sheet. And much like today, the exporters receive export returns in domestic currency. The bureau, responsible to settle the payment, provides the exporter with the money in domestic currency. It can do so by getting a loan from the domestic banking system. Yet, this is precisely analogous to today's problem where surpluses involve the creation of new money. Even with the reform, the exporter is provided with money in domestic currency that did not exist before. While this new money today is provided to the payee directly by the banking system, it involves an additional loop via the bureau once the reform is in place. As we have discussed, such additional money creation, which is not related to the production of output in the domestic economy, may lead to financial bubbles by pushing up asset prices.

To prevent this, the bureau issues bonds in domestic currency. The macroeconomic effect of this step is straightforward: the buyers of these new bonds provide the bureau with the money it can use to repay the loan it was granted by the domestic banking system. The amount of money that was newly created is destroyed again. There is no bubble-driving extra money such that monetary stability in the domestic economy is ensured.[8] Towards the domestic economy, the payment is now finalized

---

[8] Some countries apply this measure even today. When an economy faces strong financial inflows that tend to drive up prices of real and financial assets, the central bank issues bonds in order to

in real terms. The country exports goods and receives bonds in exchange for it. Again, the latter represent a claim on real economic output.

Finally, the surplus of the country considered in this example is equal to the deficit of the rest of the world that we summarize as a single deficit country. The latter is about to make a double payment much like any deficit country currently does (assuming that it is not the originator of a global key currency). To prevent this, the bureau purchases financial assets abroad. This means that the bureau takes the responsibility to avoid the double payment of the external deficit of the country it trades with. Thereby, the deficit country receives foreign currency (generally speaking: reserve currency) in exchange for the financial assets sold to the surplus country such that it can balance its current account. Moreover, the country of the foreign importer is provided with the money in its own currency, which it would lose otherwise. This ensures that demand in the rest of the world can be maintained. The analogy to the global version of the payment reform thus is complete.

The final result of the payment is that the bureau has foreign securities on the asset side and bonds on the liability side of its balance sheet. This means that the foreign securities are eventually owned by the owners of the domestic bonds. The overall payment now is real: the current account imbalance is equilibrated by a transfer of securities from the deficit country to the surplus country.

Example

To explain the case of a surplus country, and to better understand the overall reform, we proceed again step by step even though the sequence may also be altered:

1. The foreign importer pays in foreign currency. The bureau receives the payment.
2. The bureau borrows from the domestic banking system to make a payment in domestic currency to the exporter.
3. The bureau now has a balance sheet that looks as follows: it has foreign reserves on its asset side and domestic debt of an equal amount on its liability side.
4. Due to the payment to the exporter, the amount of money in the domestic economy has increased. The bureau issues bonds denominated in domestic currency. It uses the money it receives therewith to repay the domestic loan. The amount of money in the economy thus is back to the initial level.
5. The bureau uses the foreign reserves to buy bonds or other securities abroad. The amount of money in the rest of the World or in the importing country, respectively, which has been reduced due to the double payment, thus is also back to the initial level.

---

reduce available liquidity and, hence, speculative pressure in the economy. This is called 'sterilization' of financial flows.

6. The bureau's final balance sheet looks as follows: on the asset side, it owns securities in foreign currency, which are matched by bonds in domestic currency on the liability side.

7. As a little extension, let us assume the case where the country ran a deficit in the past but now has turned to a net exporter resulting in a current account surplus. Then the preceding two steps can be adjusted whereas their logic remains the same: instead of issuing new bonds in domestic currency, the bureau may also repurchase those it had disposed of abroad when it was in deficit. It can resell those securities in the domestic financial market.

Whether a country runs an external deficit or a surplus, the one-country reform of international payments provides monetary stability. Particularly for developing countries, the reform allows for economic development patterns like this one: in the initial phase, the development strategy aims at increasing investment in order to steer productivity growth. The import of capital goods entails external deficits. The latter provide the bureau with extra profits, which contribute to investment in the domestic economy while the exchange rate remains stable. Improved and enlarged production capacity enables the stepwise establishment of export sectors and makes the country more competitive in international trade. Over time, the country can become a net exporter. By contrast to the current situation, however, there is no pressure at any time to achieve an external surplus because foreign debt does not build up anymore.

7.6 Making Capital Flight Harmless

All essential elements of the reform of international payments have been explained and drafted by now. From this it follows that the reformed system can cope with capital flight. However, since we have argued that it is a very central feature of developing countries' macroeconomic challenges, we emphasize its impact in a reformed payment system in some detail here. Even though the exchange rate is stabilized, capital flight may still take place when the government of a developing country starts implementing measures, which favor long-term development but jeopardize capital interests. Yet, in a reformed system, it does not have the same impact anymore.

The impact of capital outflows can be analyzed like any payment from the domestic economy to another country. The main difference is that there are neither import goods in exchange for the payment nor is the money used for specific investments abroad. Let us assume a rich resident of a country wants to transfer her money to a foreign country and hence gives her bank a payment order. The bank makes the payment implying that the bureau receives this money in domestic currency. The wealth owner is endowed with foreign currency on a bank account he has opened in a foreign bank. As with any such payment, the bureau has to get indebted in order to be able to make the payment in foreign currency. It eliminates this foreign debt by selling securities abroad while reinvesting the money it received from the wealth owner's domestic account in the national economy. The mechanism is identical to the case of the deficit country as represented in Fig. 7.1.

The most important difference to today's system is that after the reform, capital flight does not cause currency depreciation anymore. The exchange rate is set by the bureau or by the central bank such that capital flight, itself being speculative transactions, cannot impact it via the foreign exchange market anymore. Fine, one may argue, but is it not that the central bank can already do the same with the current system? It can access foreign currency via debt, or use its currency reserves, and sell it in the foreign exchange market to defend the value of the domestic currency in the sense of exchange rate pegging. Yet, this policy would meet its limits as soon as currency reserves are gone or when international creditors lose confidence in lending to the economy in trouble. They would demand higher interest rates on their loans in order to cover the higher risk. Sooner or later, this system would break down entailing massive currency devaluation and possibly hyperinflation while external debt will be a burden for the economy for decades.

This argument is true but only for exchange rate pegging. It shows a lack of understanding of the difference between pegged exchange rates and our fundamental reform of international payments. There are several reasons why the reformed system is actually able to guarantee macroeconomic stability. First, since there is no foreign exchange market anymore, speculators cannot put pressure on the exchange rate. This is what they currently do during financial crises to challenge exchange rate pegs of central banks. The exchange rate now is controlled by the bureau. Currency depreciations usually trigger further capital flight that depreciates the exchange rate further. Wealth owners even anticipate devaluations. By aiming to bring their money in security in advance, they trigger the devaluation they fear. Such a vicious cycle, itself one of the most important reasons for capital flight, is ruled out thanks to the reform.

Second, even with a pegged exchange rate, payments for current account deficits are made twice. With the reform, double payment is avoided. The bureau has to issue securities in the foreign market. But at the same time it gets hold of the money in domestic currency. Thus, the economy is not deprived of any resources. By contrast, reinvestment of this money by the bureau strengthens the productive base of the economy. On the one hand, capital flight does not have the same punishment power anymore implying that countries do not have to fear it. On the other hand, capital flight does not leave the economy behind weaker and weaker like a sinking ship as can be the case with the dynamics of today's system. This is another reason why capital flight is not self-accelerating anymore.

These reasons, which distinguish the one-country reform from the instruments a central bank has at its disposal now, do not allow capital flight to break down an economy anymore. Wealth owners may move their money out of the country, but the country does not lose any resources. It can keep up productive activity and expand it via investment.

Let us put it like this in a simple stylized case: capital in its broadest sense means ownership of assets, be it physically or via equity, debt or bank deposits. If a capitalist decides to move wealth abroad, he has to turn it into liquid form such that it can be transferred to a foreign economy. Since the bureau receives the domestic currency from the payment, it can buy those real or financial assets sold by the capitalist. By now, the capitalist's wealth is represented as a deposit in a foreign bank. He can use it to buy the financial securities, which are supplied to the foreign country by the bureau and, in the simplest case, represent a claim on the assets purchased by the bureau. The capitalist thus ends up owning the same assets as he did when his wealth was in the domestic economy.

Needless to say, neither is the capitalist forced to buy the bureau's bonds nor does the bureau necessarily have to purchase the assets left by the capitalist. Both agents can acquire other assets while the domestic assets left by the capitalist and the deficit economy's securities can be bought by other agents as well. However, the book-keeping in this example shows how the reform ensures monetary and economic stability despite capital flight.

References

Brunette C (2015) External debt duplication: effect of a payment system aberration. Ph.D. thesis, Università Svizzera Italiana. https://isidore.science/document/10670/1.da43zi

OECD (2020) COVID-19 and global capital flows. https://read.oecd-ilibrary.org/view/?ref=134_134881-twep75dnkt&title=COVID-19-and-global-capital-flows.   Accessed 15 Apr 2021

Rossi S (2015) Structural reforms in payment systems to avoid another systemic crisis. Rev Keynesian Econ 3(2):213–225. https://doi.org/10.4337/roke.2015.02.05

Schmitt B (2014) The formation of sovereign debt: diagnosis and remedy. http://papers.ssrn.com/sol3/papers.cfm?abstract_id=2513679

Schumacher EF (1943) Multilateral clearing. Economica, New Series 10(38):150–165

Varoufakis Y, Halevi J, Theocarakis NJ (2011) Modern political economics: making sense of the post-2008 world. Routledge, New York

Chapter 8
Macroeconomics for Development

Throughout the past chapters, this book has gathered the elements of various areas that we need in order to provide the macroeconomic bottom line for long-term development and poverty reduction. We have seen that waiting for markets to bring about higher living standards in developing countries cannot work. Mainstream economics tells us all the details about efficient markets but misses to tell the whole story of capitalism, which does not only include exchange in the marketplace but also money creation and a production process. Both effective demand and a sufficient profit rate are conditions for economic development to take place.

An effective development strategy requires policy intervention. Income redistribution via taxing and social transfers help strengthen effective demand. In the long term, poor countries need to foster investment in order to create larger production capacity. The state needs to target sectors, which are important from a macroeconomic and social point of view. In contrast to private investment, public investment does not rely on profitability but can also sustain deficits for quite a long time. Areas with particularly high investment needs are, among many others, infrastructure or the processing of primary goods in order to increase the value of exports. Active economic policy should pursue an industrialization defined in a broad sense (see for instance Cramer et al. 2020, pp. 98–107).

To provide finance for such investment projects, developing countries can create national development banks or, in countries where they already exist, strengthen their position. A lack of money is never the problem. Neither the public nor the private sector are prevented from increasing economic activity by money scarcity. Money can be provided upon demand. The problems for the private sector are profitability and demand. The reason why a single firm does not invest in a developing country is that the investment does not yield sufficient profits. It could increase prices in order to have a better margin, which then makes the goods unaffordable for the population with low income, hence the problem of insufficient demand.

The public sector is not subject to this constraint. National development banks are equal in this regard. They do not rely on profits and therefore can provide loans at

© Springer Fachmedien Wiesbaden GmbH, part of Springer Nature 2022
B. Oberholzer, *Fighting Global Poverty*, SpringerBriefs in Economics,
https://doi.org/10.1007/978-3-658-36631-5_8

lower interest rates if required from the point of view of the government's development strategy. In this way, neither the government nor the bank as the source of finance claim a part of output in the form of interest. Therefore, such a growth strategy can exclusively focus on demand as a condition for economic prosperity. When generating employment in the public sector, the corresponding income creation is tantamount to the demand required to ensure economic expansion.

For a poor country, designing a development strategy involves trade-offs. Money is not limited but real resources such as technology and specialized workforce are. Endogenous money thus is not a panacea that by itself is sufficient to guarantee full employment and increasing living standards. In macroeconomics, money creation is better perceived as a supporting mechanism that allows for development strategies, which would otherwise be unfeasible. Since real resources are the bottleneck, it may thus be necessary to concentrate resources in sectors, which are identified as being of high priority. Such selection cannot be achieved by the market because the only thing the market does is allocating resources where profitability and demand currently are sufficient. This can easily lead to inefficient use of resources, thus harming productivity growth in the long term. Even worse, market forces waste a lot of resources and production potential, among which mainly the workforce, by leaving it idle.

Public investment creates employment and helps pull people out of the precarious informal sector. In poor countries where the informal sector covers the vast majority of the population, full employment in a formal sense is hardly achievable in one decade or two. But employment can be strongly increased. Moreover, by setting conditions in the public sector right, the private sector can also be influenced. Mainly by driving effective demand and the profit rate, the government can achieve a crowding-in of the private sector, thus multiplying its own efforts. In particular, by increasing productivity, for example due to improved infrastructure or energy production, profitability conditions for private firms can be much brighter.

Additionally, the legal setting of a minimum wage is another steering instrument. Moreover, the government can decide at which wage rate it hires workers. This wage rate is a benchmark that influences the private sector via altered bargaining powers in the labor market. Depending on growth being wage-led or profit-led, setting a higher wage can be beneficial to or dragging economic performance.

A development strategy containing these elements would not be feasible if we still faced a balance of payments constraint. Countries with external deficits, especially those punished by capital flight, experience currency devaluation, inflation and growing external debt. However, by complementing domestic economic policy with the one-country reform of international payments, the external constraint is removed. Developing countries then are allowed to run current account deficits, which enables them to build up improved production plants. Thanks to the reform and the installment of a bureau as a settlement agency and a domestic investor, a country can avoid the flaws of the current international payment system.

With the reform of international payments, a country gains back control over its exchange rate. As part of the development strategy, the central bank can set the exchange rate at a level deemed as appropriate. This involves considerations of international competitiveness on the one hand and domestic demand and income on the other hand.

In this context, institutional aspects should be taken into account. Many important institutions in developing countries are often quite weak. Economic policies can only be considered as appropriate, if they take these weaknesses into account. This means that if we find that they rely on too complicated requirements with regard to practical implementation, they are probably not feasible. The one-country reform should pass the test quite well. The bureau is the only new institution to be established as part of the reform. It can be integrated into a specific department of the government or be created as a more independent entity. In any case, it is a public institution. Its most demanding task is the reinvestment of the extra profits. The general government already has a more or less ambitious investment plan so that institutional capacity should be available at least partially.

All other agents, except the banks, do not even notice the reform if they do not know about it. As long as domestic banks comply with the prescription that they are allowed to have neither assets nor liabilities in foreign currency on their balance sheets, the implementation of the reform is straightforward. There is no incentive for circumvention. For instance, speculators could think about exchanging currency against another one at an exchange rate differing from the bureau's one. Yet, closer consideration shows that this does not undermine the bureau's authority as the setter of the exchange rate. Whether currency is offered at a higher or lower rate, there is always one party in the exchange, which is better off by making the payment via the bureau.

With the reform, capital controls are basically not necessary anymore because the bureau can deal with international financial flows. However, there can be circumstances when capital outflows are too high for all the extra profits arising from the external deficit to be invested in a meaningful way. A development plan goes through different stages. Too high investment at a time may be more than the domestic economy can handle due to, for example, the impact on the labor market where there might be a shortage of specific experts.

A similar argument applies to tariffs. If trade deficits grow to a level where extra profits of the bureau are far higher than needed or manageable, tariffs can be a way to keep the deficit under control. This could be wishful as there may be political reasons not to give up too many of the domestic real resources to guarantee the functioning of the reform in the deficit case. Hence, whereas the one-country reform of international payments provides the bottom line for a developing country's relationship to the rest of the world, capital controls and tariffs may be additional tools to be applied in specific situations. Yet, beyond the impact on the balance of payments, tariffs may still be useful for infant industry protection as has been argued above.

Box 8.1   The East Asian Development Experience

The numbers on poverty and the state of development in Latin America, Africa and Asia at the beginning of this book reveal how difficult it is to actually measure people's wellbeing and quality of life. But they are at least able to show that on these three continents, East Asia is the only region, which has experienced an unambiguous steady increase in living standards since the middle of the past century.[1] For instance, whereas the share of Chinese in the poorest 10% of world population (measured by income) was 58% in 1981, it was only 11% in 2010 (Woodward 2015, p. 53). According to the common policy prescriptions by mainstream economics including the multilateral finance institutions like the World Bank and the International Monetary Fund, this success can only be explained by East Asian countries' free-market policies. These prescriptions entail privatization of public assets, liberalization of trade and financial flows, deregulation of domestic financial markets, and a minimized role for the state. To achieve those development goals, both conservative fiscal and monetary policies are needed in order to not distort market dynamics.

However, a closer look easily reveals that the successful countries—independent of whether oriented towards the West or not—have pursued development strategies that assign a prominent role to the state.[2] Countries like Taiwan and South Korea had quite large sectors of state-owned enterprises during their decades of highest growth and performed much better than many Latin American countries where the corresponding shares were lower. It is by no means that the public sector is inevitably inefficient. By contrast, many public enterprises in these countries faced competition with the private sector domestically and in the world market. In this sense, it is also not surprising that East Asian countries made active use of industrial policy to coordinate economic resources and make long-term investments neglected by private companies as well as target selected sectors for these investments. Those sectors received subsidized loans from public banks to have better starting conditions. Moreover, large-scale research and development expenditures were made to support sectoral development.

Naturally, this policy set also included so-called 'infant industry protection' and hence active trade policies applying tariffs. New industries needed to be protected for efficiency gains from learning processes to materialize. Moreover, government support allowed for establishing industries at a size at which

(continued)

---

[1] While Japan's period of strong growth already started in the 1960s, China's was initiated later in the 1970s.

[2] For a broader account on the East Asian economic success story, see Chang (2006) and Wade (1990).

Box 8.1 (continued)

economies of scale reduced unit costs of production. Pressure on the managements of these public-owned companies by the government was quite high in order to ensure that sufficient productivity progress makes them competitive in the world market.

Before the period of liberalization, capital controls were a conventional instrument to limit sudden capital inflows and outflows. They also helped direct investment and prevented that capital would flow to sectors, and hence allocate economic resources, that were not of top priority to the respective national growth strategies. Likewise, control of capital outflows was the essential tool to prevent currency crises. As of today, foreign capital in China still faces rather strong legal restrictions while capital outflows are strictly controlled. For instance, any overseas payment must be reported and not exceed a certain benchmark per payer in a year. A similar objective was pursued by the application of tariffs on luxury consumption goods in South Korea. It reduced the amount of currency reserves being lost to the country due to imports of those goods and at the same time forced the elites to contribute their savings to domestic investment (Chang 2006, pp. 24–28). This again reduced the reliance on foreign capital.

Without these policies, Japan, South Korea and Taiwan would hardly have developed, among others, their famous automobile and electronics industries. To give an example, the World Bank recommended the government of South Korea in the 1960s not to go into the steel industry and neither was any private sector company willing to take this risk. Yet, the government enforced development of the steel sector with the whole set of industrial policies. POSCO was not only a successful state-owned enterprise but has come to be the third largest steel producer in the world and played a very important role in South Korea's industrialization.

What these countries had, and mostly still have, in common is the export orientation of their economies. While this strategy has the mentioned fundamental limits at a global level, it may even have become more difficult now compared to the 70s of the past century. Demand in advanced economies has tended to stagnation since the outbreak of the financial crisis in 2008 and the coronavirus pandemic as made long-term economic prospects even more uncertain. Our analysis and the suggestion of the unilateral payment reform aim to provide a solution to this bottleneck.

References

Chang H-J (2006) The east Asian development experience: the miracle, the crisis and the future. Penang, Zed Books Ltd. and Third World Network, London

Cramer C, Sender J, Oqubay A (2020) African economic development: evidence, theory, policy. Oxford University Press, Oxford

Wade RH (1990) Governing the market: economic theory and the role of government in east Asian industrialization. Princeton University Press, Princeton

Woodward D (2015) Incrementum ad absurdum: global growth, inequality and poverty eradication in a carbon-constrained world. World Econ Rev 4:43–62

Chapter 9
Economic Growth Forever?

Even though growth is not everything, it is obvious that developing countries cannot eliminate poverty but by providing higher incomes to people. An improvement in material living standards necessarily involves economic growth (see Box 2.1). However, assuming that the sketch of our macroeconomic strategy is successful, where does it eventually lead us? Is growth endless? We can imagine that at a certain living standard, continued income growth becomes nonsense. At some point, not only our basic needs are satisfied but also our interests and desire in culture, arts, sports, and other self-fulfilling activities. We then start asking the question whether it is actually not better to spend more leisure time instead of accumulating more capital goods which themselves produce goods that satisfy needs that are already overfed.

This question is quite hypothetical for developing countries but urgent to be treated in advanced economies. The reason for this is not only philosophical but also existential with regard to the environmental boundaries of our planet. Bigger output of goods and services means more consumption of energy and natural resources. Endless economic growth thus may give way to the breakdown of ecosystems and further heat up the climate up to its collapse. Quite obviously, the fight against poverty relies on a healthy environment. The value of nature is more than economical. But speaking in economic terms is one way to express nature's importance. Environmental damages reduce the availability of essential resources such as freshwater or fertile soil. This has a direct negative impact on an economy's productivity, notably in developing countries where agriculture plays a dominant role. The effects of climate change will be even much more devastating if not tackled consequently. In the twenty-first century, therefore, development macroeconomics cannot be discussed without referring to the natural environment and the potential limits of growth.

The optimistic view of economic growth claims that thanks to technological progress, our economies become more energy-efficient and we can replace fossil fuels by renewable energy, thereby stopping climate change and environmental pollution. Moreover, better technology will make sectors such as agriculture less space-consuming and soil-polluting, thus leaving more space to natural habitats.

B. Oberholzer, *Fighting Global Poverty*, SpringerBriefs in Economics,
https://doi.org/10.1007/978-3-658-36631-5_9

Whereas modern technology and increased efficiency are indispensable preconditions to achieve ecological sustainability, they are not sufficient considering the fact that global energy consumption is still growing (see Oberholzer 2017, pp. 9–12). Business as usual is not an option. Moreover, if people in today's developing countries are to get out of poverty (while still being far from the living standards of advanced economies) by supporting hitherto patterns of income distribution, global GDP would have to multiply by the factor 173 (Woodward 2015, p. 58). Even with the most optimistic scenarios of technological progress, we can simply not imagine that this can be achieved while at the same time respecting the constraints that nature sets us.

Hence, instead of promoting limitless growth, poverty reduction should be achieved via more redistribution of wealth and resources. Consequently, while growth is required in poor countries, it must be curbed once a certain living standard is achieved. Clearly, the latter applies to the currently richest nations of the world. The question naturally following from this assessment is: what does the ideal of sustainable and stagnating output and its redistribution mean for macroeconomic dynamics?

Apart from the question of how high growth is supposed to be according to these thoughts, it is equally important to look at real-world data showing how actual growth evolves. In fact, there are strong signs of global economic stagnation. Longterm economic growth in industrial countries has been falling for more than half a century now (Freeman 2019). Marx (1894/2008, pp. 209–211) provides an explanation for this observation called the 'tendency of the fall in the profit rate'. In the course of economic development, capital is accumulated. This means that the profit rate, that is, the ratio of profits to capital, tends to fall over time. Profitability of investment as one of the two key growth engines is jeopardized. The decline in the profit rate can be countered by productivity growth since higher productivity contributes to higher profits with a given capital stock. Yet, the rate of productivity progress has declined as well over the past decades and, as observation shows us, has been insufficient in generating constantly high growth rates.

One may like the decreasing-growth data as they may help the environment. Yet, capitalism would not be capitalism if it accepted reduced profitability. Investment only takes place if it yields sufficient returns. Hence, a low profit rate means less investment and, consequently, rising unemployment. To make capital profitable again, employers want to reduce production costs in order to harvest higher profits. To cut production costs, wages have to be cut accordingly. Thus, due to capital's permanent chase after profit, low economic growth entails social hardship in the form of higher unemployment and lower wages.[1] Fighting poverty without economic growth seems unachievable. Moreover, aiming at poverty reduction without growth by enforcing redistribution of incomes in an otherwise anyway stagnating environment squeezes the profit rate even more. It thus seems that we can either have

---

[1] It should be added that unemployment and falling wages give way to shrinking effective demand, which again jeopardizes economic growth as has been shown in Chap. 4.

low growth or better social conditions (far from claiming that they are perfect). But having both at the same time appears unachievable. In other words, we would like to have less growth but conventional economic policy is not able to control the resulting harmful macroeconomic dynamics and social consequences.

We can get more clarity by making one step back to Chap. 5. We have explained how markets alone cannot deliver development. The public sector is required to make investment, create employment and strengthen productivity. This is possible because the government does not rely on the profitability of its investment. Whereas at the early stage of economic development the state gets engaged in sectors where the private sector is absent, it can do exactly the same thing at the late stage. It can become active in sectors where private companies withdraw due to falling profitability and particularly in those sectors that have never been profitable so far. Specifically, public investment is needed in branches such as renewable energy production that are key for ecological transformation. Since profitability is not required, the government can focus on the second macroeconomic condition, that is, the maintenance of effective demand. Thereby, it is able to keep production and employment on desired levels while there is no need to put downward pressure on wages. Once a sufficient share of economic activity is run by the public sector, output of the economy can be kept stable so that there is no necessity to grow further.

While government action in developing countries is expected to achieve a high growth rate via crowding-in of the private sector, the opposite applies at a later stage of economic development. Now, the public sector does not make investment and create employment in order to increase wealth as a first priority. It rather expands to new areas neglected by the private sector in order to maintain employment and providing those goods of high social need. By keeping employment high, the government can drive wages. Higher wages shrink the profit rate and imply a crowding-out of the private sector. Harmful at the beginning of economic development, crowding-out may actually be a powerful mechanism to transform more advanced economies into systems, which are to the benefit of human needs and ecological sustainability rather than profit.

To the extent that productivity increases year after year, the result in the new regime is not just faster accumulation of capital and expansion of production. Instead, now it becomes possible to reduce working time at the favor of leisure with output remaining the same. Beyond this, the transformation outlined here allows for working time reduction even in the absence of productivity growth. In such a case, decreasing working time would go along with decreasing income. Society would be free to decide on the level of working time with a corresponding income level. The main difference to capitalism as we know it today is the guarantee of macroeconomic stability thanks to public sector production. Currently, a (substantial) reduction in working time involves unforeseen turbulences and most likely a profit squeeze and hence unemployment. For working time reduction to be possible with stable employment, a transformative macroeconomic framework is required.

Public sector production not only allows for stability but can also drive growth at a rate that is still considered as appropriate and sustainable. In several sectors such as renewable energy, expansion is a requirement while output in unsustainable sectors should be curbed. A transformation driven by public sector investment and employment does not necessarily involve permanent degrowth. The fundamental change consists in the fact that growth is not a systemic imperative anymore. Instead, economic policy has the freedom to decide on the rate of growth without being exposed to systemic forces of permanent growth.

Such a transformative path to a growth-independent economy is quite far away for developing countries. Moreover, it involves a lot of uncertainties and still unknown effects. But the fight against poverty on the one hand and economic transformation on the other hand have a common feature: they require scope of action for economic policy. They have active economic policy intervention at its center in order to guide the patterns of employment, investment and accumulation. Finally, to both of the challenges—economic development to overcome poverty and transformation to a growth-independent economy—it applies that an appropriate system of international payments creates the macroeconomic and monetary stability needed for such purposes.

References

Freeman A (2019) The sixty-year downward trend of economic growth in the industrialised countries of the world. GERG Data Group Working Paper, no. 1. https://www.academia.edu/38192121/The_sixty_year_downward_trend_of_economic_growth_in_the_industrialised_countries_of_the_world. Accessed 10 Oct 2020

Marx K (1894/2004) Das Kapital. Kritik der politischen Ökonomie, dritter Band. Akademie Verlag, Berlin

Oberholzer B (2017) Monetary policy and crude oil: prices, production and consumption. Edward Elgar, Cheltenham and Northampton

Woodward D (2015) Incrementum ad absurdum: global growth, inequality and poverty eradication in a carbon-constrained world. World Econ Rev 4:43–62

Chapter 10
New Perspectives

To reduce poverty, and therefore also inequality, progressive strategies are needed. Economic policy based on market intervention, redistribution and public investment must be part of such a project. However, it can only be successful, if policy action gets a chance to be implemented. As long as capitalist dynamics punish progressive governments through capital flight as well as macroeconomic instability and crisis, they are much likely doomed to failure. Moreover, countries must be allowed to run current account deficits in order to build the economy's productive capacity. The latter requires a period of large-scale investment involving imports of capital goods and technology. Likewise, feeding basic needs or, for example, bridging droughts give way to external deficits before a country is able to manage these challenges out of its own resources. A poor country must be able to sustain such periods without running into a currency crisis.

Today, many countries do not even think about a different way of doing economic policy because the threat of a painful reaction of global financial markets is pre-eminent. Mainstream policy prescriptions then are what is left. Governments have to keep expenditures low since otherwise they would cause current account deficits. They have to run constant external surpluses or at least a balanced current account, which means they mostly rely on the existing export sectors that produce primary commodities. Also, the countries cannot adopt any policies that would scare wealth owners as this would induce capital flight. Moreover, to the extent that a country runs a current account deficit, it relies on capital inflows to finance it. Hence, it has to implement particularly capital-friendly policies such that the financial flows keep coming.

The reform of international payments presented in this book allows developing countries to run current account deficits and to pursue alternative development patterns without triggering exchange rate depreciation and currency crisis. They have their scope of action back to successfully pursue a progressive development strategy. In particular, the countries get the chance to drive economic development not according to the needs of capital's profitability but of society's needs.

© Springer Fachmedien Wiesbaden GmbH, part of Springer Nature 2022
B. Oberholzer, *Fighting Global Poverty*, SpringerBriefs in Economics,
https://doi.org/10.1007/978-3-658-36631-5_10

One may argue that East Asian countries were successful without such a reform. Indeed, they applied many instruments of economic policy, which can give a good example to today's poorest countries in Latin America, Africa and the rest of Asia. As Box 8.1 has shown, the East Asian development plans largely ignored policy recommendations of the economic mainstream, which allowed them to achieve the longest-lasting and fastest process in economic development in human history. True, however, they also did it without such a reform.

But times were quite different when the East Asian success stories started. Global growth is lower today and we have experienced more than three decades of liberalization in trade and capital flows. Capitalism has definitely become more instable, particularly since 2008 and the subsequent stagnation that is still lasting. In 2020, the coronavirus crisis hit the global economy at a scale that led to the strongest drop in global economic growth since the Great Depression in the 1930s. Foreign debt in developing countries that had already been high before took off even faster. The now sluggish global growth thus is likely to see another long-term downturn.

With global growth stagnating, developing countries face a lot of constraints in pursuing an export-led growth model. Moreover, industrialization may not be as much a straightforward strategy as it once was. With the technological progress evolving, conventional industrial development in a country may reach its peak sooner and at a lower level today compared to the advanced economies when they were at the respective stages of development. Even though industrialization remains an important objective with the manufacturing sector being an essential engine of growth, service sectors most probably will play a more important role also for developing countries. This might again set conditions for export-led growth regimes tighter. Overall, conditions for a poor country's economic development are less favorable than they were in the second half of the twentieth century. The reclaim of more freedom in the current account as provided by the unilateral reform of international payments, thus is crucial.

The previous chapter exhibited the connection between economic development on the one hand and the general connection between economic growth, living standards and the natural environment on the other hand in order to ask the question about the future of growth. We outlined a strategy of how the economy may become growth-independent. Economic development of poor countries and long-term macroeconomic transformation to sustainability share a common feature. To the extent that the respective strategies are to be implemented by a government of an individual country, they rely on economic and thus political autonomy and sovereignty. Therefore, the importance of a reform, which removes the external constraint, cannot be overestimated. In a world of global competition where it is completely uncertain if cooperation among countries can be achieved at any meaningful time horizon, the option for a single country to move forward is key to any economic progress.

This statement may be challenged by arguing that economics is not the only obstacle to successful development. There are wars, historical and ethnic conflicts, rigged elections, different cultures and ways of life and much more that this book has not taken into account. And in particular, countries are ruled by corrupt elites who do not have the least interest in lifting their people out of misery. So why and how should a development strategy as outlined here ever be implemented?

True, economics is not everything. It is interwoven with numerous other disciplines jointly representing a reality far more complex than assumed here. And corruption is one of the most frustrating problems and part of daily life in developing countries. Clearly, there are political barriers and elites who do everything to avoid more social justice. But this does not change anything about the fact that even when there is a progressive government seriously trying to improve the poor's situation, the economic constraints are too tight. Such well-meaning governments have been in place many times throughout history and around the planet. However, capitalist turbulences were a main cause of their failure. Given that progressive policies get a chance of success thanks to the systemic changes described here, their track record may change to the positive. Success stories of economic development can be shared. And they raise pressure on corrupt elites because they know there are viable alternatives to challenge them. We urgently need development strategies whose success gives a leading example to other countries. They would change perspectives for the poor of the world.

Lightning Source UK Ltd.
Milton Keynes UK
UKHW030729180322
400272UK00005B/358